·The Missionary·

·The Missionary·
Michael Palin

Methuen

First published in Great Britain 1983
by Methuen London Ltd, 11 New Fetter Lane, London EC4P 4EE
Copyright © 1983 Hand Made Films (1981) Partnership

Designed by Pat Gavin and Terry Griffiths
Photographs: Hand Made Films; David Farrell

Printed in Great Britain
by Blantyre Printing and Binding Co. Ltd, Glasgow

British Library Cataloguing in Publication Data

Palin, Michael
  The missionary.
  I. Title
  791.43'72   PN1997.M/

  ISBN 0-413-51010-7
  ISBN 0-413-51390-4 Pbk

There had been many legendary white men in nineteenth-century Africa. There was 'Mad Arnold' Frobisher who used to attack crocodiles for no reason at all. There was the Reverend Cyril Toogood who walked forty miles before breakfast every day, and died of starvation after three weeks. There was 'Chief' Arthur Wallington, a solicitor from Weymouth who turned native and took the name Odaka Ohuru Na ('the solicitor from Weymouth'), and 'Wee Jackie' Venables-King, a district commissioner in Ngara Province who died trying to carve his initials on a sleeping rhino. There were men of courage and remarkable tenacity – like Jocelyn Onan-Smythe, the first man to take a touring company of *The Yeomen of the Guard* over the Zambesi Falls, and Nigel Quiverton whose ambitious plan to irrigate the Sahara Desert failed when one of his two barrels sprang a leak. Into this world came Charles Fortescue, a promising young clergyman who left Southampton for East Africa in 1896. Like those before him, Fortescue was no ordinary man. Just how extraordinary he was, our tale will tell . . .

An English public school, 1907.

A splendid, carefully maintained Gothick honours board, with a list of names in gold lettering under the heading 'ST ANSELM'S SCHOOL. HONOURS 1880–1906'.

There is the sound of a tolling bell and boys' footsteps on stone passageways making their way to chapel. An aged school painter approaches the board, sets down some steps and a wooden case of paints and brushes.

The tolling has stopped, so has the sound of the boys in the passageways. A door slams. An organ is heard playing the first two lines of 'From Greenland's Icy Mountains'. The school painter directs his brush at the honours board. The organ introduction dies away. His paintbrush slowly and deliberately wipes out the name 'Fortescue C. W. 1889–1894'.

At that moment a full-throated school congregation begins the classic hymn.

SCHOOL CONGREGATION *(off)*. From Greenland's icy mountains
                             From India's coral strand . . .
                             From Africa's sunny fountains . . .

Africa. March 1906.

A scorpion arches its back and scuttles away. A grubby hand makes a grab for it. Misses.

In a small, fly-ridden mud-walled church in Kenya a missionary, the REVEREND CHARLES FORTESCUE, *is enthusiastically playing away on a small battered portable missionary-issue harmonium. A group of Africans are singing along with him. They take up the hymn we have heard at the school.*

AFRICAN CONGREGATION *(singing lustily)*. ... Roll down their golden sand
　　　　　　　　　　　　　　　From many an ancient river,
　　　　　　　　　　　　　　　From many a palmy plain ...

The boy chasing the scorpion is now crawling around between FORTESCUE *and the organ.* FORTESCUE *stops him with a sharp but humane slap on the head and sends him back to the congregation.*

AFRICAN CONGREGATION *(singing)*. They call us to deliver
　　　　　　　　　　　　　　　Their land from error's chain.

Over images of the dark mysterious, primitive side of Africa the congregation warble on.

AFRICAN CONGREGATION. What though the spicy breezes
　　　　　　　　　　　　　Blow soft o'er Java's isle,
　　　　　　　　　　　　　Though every prospect pleases
　　　　　　　　　　　　　And only man is vile;

　　　　　　　　　　　　　In vain with lavish kindness
　　　　　　　　　　　　　The gifts of God are strown;
　　　　　　　　　　　　　The heathen in his blindness
　　　　　　　　　　　　　Bows down to wood and stone.

　　　　　　　　　　　　　Can we, whose souls are lighted
　　　　　　　　　　　　　With wisdom from on high,
　　　　　　　　　　　　　Can we to men benighted
　　　　　　　　　　　　　The lamp of life deny? ...

In burning red sunsets, beneath thorn trees or amongst the mud huts we see the MISSIONARY *amongst his people. Joining in with their way of life – helping to cut reeds, helping to thatch a house, teaching them the rudiments of cricket, walking with the cattle, at a makeshift surgery.*

There is an unforced, spontaneous delight in each other's company between mission and missionary. Amongst these images is a recurring one of a little black girl running with a letter. She runs out of a trading post across scrubland and arid hard-baked earth towards the mountain of Ololokwe, beneath which is the mud chapel from which rises the sound of the African congregation.

AFRICAN CONGREGATION. Salvation! O salvation!
                  The joyful sound proclaim . . .

The girl bursts into the church. FORTESCUE *looks up as she pushes her way through the cheerful congregation. She forces her way through to the front, bows briefly before the stained glass window made out of old bottles and hands* FORTESCUE *the letter.*

AFRICAN CONGREGATION. Till each remotest nation . . .
                  Has learned Messiah's name.

The organ runs down and dies as FORTESCUE *sees the letter. His face clouds. He takes the letter and opens it with an air of inevitability. Quickly he scans the contents, his face falls. He looks at the expectant, eager congregation and down at the little girl. His face is full of sadness. The little African girl smiles back up at him.*

𝐀 *passenger/cargo boat in the English Channel. Late April 1906.*

NARRATOR. In the spring of 1906 after ten years of selfless service in some of the most inhospitable corners of Britain's far-flung Empire, Charles Fortescue, the missionary, returned to England, a hero.

The boat is approaching the white cliffs of Dover on a very grey and rainy day. Wind lashes the deck on which travellers returning to England from the far-flung corners of the Empire are gathering.

Edging his way to the front of the group, who are pointing excitedly at the white cliffs, is our missionary. He is clutching, with some difficulty, two suitcases and a variety of phallic African tribal objects.

The boat lurches suddenly and FORTESCUE *drops his tribal objects. One, a small polished skull, rolls under the rail.*

FORTESCUE *makes a grab for it, and as he bends down one of the long curving African objects embeds itself in a tall, elegant, beautiful, dark-eyed lady standing behind him.*

FORTESCUE *whirls round apologetically.*

FORTESCUE. I'm terribly sorry ...!

ELEGANT LADY *(holding her hat on against the wind)*. Don't worry ... *(She smiles.)* ... I'm not hurt. Taken by surprise, that's all ...

FORTESCUE. They're rather difficult to, er ... handle ...

He scrabbles around on the deck, stopping one with his foot. She bends down and picks it up for him.

ELEGANT LADY. Especially in this weather ...

FORTESCUE. Yes ... it doesn't help ...

ELEGANT LADY. What are they ...?

FORTESCUE. Er ... fertility objects ... African ...

An elderly colonel figure bends down and retrieves another object.

FORTESCUE. ... Oh thank you, thank you so much, you're very kind.

ELEGANT LADY. They're beautiful.

FORTESCUE. Yes, well, sexual potency is frightfully important out there ...

The rest of the respectable crowd who hear this react in some shock at the boldness of his language. He is, after all, a man of the cloth.

The ELEGANT LADY *smiles a little enigmatically as she notices this reaction.*

ELEGANT LADY. Well, welcome home, Mr Fortescue.

FORTESCUE. Thank you ... er ... and you are M ...?

Another blast from the ship's siren breaks the moment of intimacy and causes FORTESCUE *to drop yet another well-rounded African totem. He retrieves it and looks up eagerly. But the* ELEGANT LADY *is gone.*

Rural Oxfordshire. A coach and pair bumps through a pretty stretch of English woodland. Sun-dappled light through beech trees. All that nonsense.

Inside sit FORTESCUE *and a cheerful, reassuring, avuncular parson — the* REVEREND FITZBANKS.

FITZBANKS. You look terribly well, dear boy . . . How was it out there, frightful?

FORTESCUE. No, not half bad, sir . . .

FITZBANKS. Any cannibalism?

FORTESCUE. Not where I was, no . . .

FITZBANKS *(faintly disappointed)*. Ah . . . People eaten *near* you, I suppose.

FORTESCUE. No . . .

FITZBANKS. Atrocities?

FORTESCUE. Not to speak of . . . no, sir.

FITZBANKS *(sadly)*. Oh, well . . . One hears such dreadful stories . . .

FORTESCUE. How is . . . Deborah?

FITZBANKS. Oh, she's just like a little child, you know . . . Terribly excited . . .

FORTESCUE. Well, she *was* a child when I left.

FITZBANKS. She's a fine woman now. By God's grace the image of her mother.

FORTESCUE. Yes, I was very sorry to hear about Mrs Fitzbanks.

FITZBANKS. The Lord giveth . . . and the Lord taketh away.

FORTESCUE. She loved ice-skating, I remember.

FITZBANKS. Yes . . . it was her life, bless her.

The coach clatters down a picturesque hill towards the idyllic little village of Little Fidding, past the village green, past the famous one-eyed postman, and into the driveway of a crumbling old rectory. PARSWELL *the coachman reins the horses to a halt rather too abruptly. The tribal treasures roll off the roof and on to the gravel.*

FITZBANKS. Steady, Parswell!

PARSWELL. Sorry, sir...

FITZBANKS *and* FORTESCUE *climb out.* FORTESCUE *looks around expectantly. A mangy dog shuffles out of the house, accompanied by rich insect life.*

FORTESCUE. Surely this can't be old Major?

The dog hobbles up to FORTESCUE, *who bends to pat it.*

FORTESCUE *(with a chuckle).* He still remembers me...! Hello, old boy!

MAJOR *waddles past, totally ignoring him.*

PARSWELL *is struggling to collect the African objects; he keeps picking one up and dropping another.*

FITZBANKS. Come on, Parswell... I'll give you a hand. What are these anyway?

FORTESCUE. Fertility symbols mainly. They knew I was going to marry, you see...

FITZBANKS *(aside to Parswell).* Better not show them to Deborah – take them up the back stairs, all right...?

Expectantly FORTESCUE *enters the dark hallway of the rectory. It's low-ceilinged and wood-panelled.*

FORTESCUE. Deborah! Deborah!... I'm back.

He turns as a door opens on the far side of the hall. A beautiful, dark-eyed young girl dressed in a simple dark shift appears.

FORTESCUE's *mouth opens in amazement.*

FORTESCUE. Deborah... You look *absolutely* marvellous...

GIRL *(shyly).* I'm Emily, the maid, sir...

FORTESCUE. Oh... oh... er... sorry...

EMILY. I'll help bring your things in, sir...

FORTESCUE *(in some confusion).* Er... yes... yes... they're outside.

EMILY *curtsies and goes out.*

A rather firmer, heartier, more well-rounded upper-class female voice is heard from the top of the stairs.

GIRL'S VOICE. Hello Charles...

He looks up. Standing there is a rather pretty, open-faced young girl. She obviously doesn't care overmuch for her appearance, but has a rosy, innocent glow to her skin, and a flush of excitement in her cheeks.

FORTESCUE *(a little tentatively this time)*. Deborah . . . ?

There is a slight, embarrassed pause – as though he should have added something more, but couldn't think of anything to say.

FORTESCUE. Well . . . er . . . how are you?

DEBORAH. Oh, ever so well. How are you?

FORTESCUE. Not so bad . . . Twenty-six days at sea . . . I feel a bit like an unpacked bag.

DEBORAH. I can get you one if you want.

FORTESCUE. No . . . No. I feel as if I *am* one.

DEBORAH. Oh!

She laughs, a trifle horsily. They both laugh. This breaks the ice a little. They go towards each other, a little stiffly, to meet at the bottom of the stairs.

DEBORAH. Charles?

FORTESCUE *(eagerly)*. Yes.

DEBORAH. There's some lunch.

FORTESCUE *(smiling at her for a moment)*. It's been such a long time.

DEBORAH. Yes, well, I didn't know when you would be arriving.

FORTESCUE. Since we last saw each other.

DEBORAH. Oh . . . oh, yes . . .

FORTESCUE. Ten years . . .

DEBORAH. Ten years, four months, eighteen days, twenty-five minutes . . .

They both smile . . . FORTESCUE *starts towards her as if to embrace her.*

DEBORAH *(moving)*. It's cold . . .

FORTESCUE. What?

DEBORAH. The lunch.

FORTESCUE. Oh . . . oh . . . oh, that's lovely.

He follows her towards the dining-room.

FORTESCUE. It's just . . . so good to be back.

DEBORAH. I hope you're hungry.

FORTESCUE. Rather. Haven't eaten since the Bay of Biscay.

Later, in the dining-room, DEBORAH, FORTESCUE *and the* REVEREND FITZBANKS *sit round a table, which groans with pies, hams, kedgeree, chicken legs etc. arrayed most temptingly.* FITZBANKS *is in the middle of a long Latin grace.*

FITZBANKS. Oculi omnium in te spectant, Domine.
        Et tu das illis escam in tempore.
        Aperis tu manum tuam;
        Et imples omnia animalia benedictione tua.

FORTESCUE *looks up and makes for the food, only to realise with some embarrassment that* FITZBANKS *has not finished.*

FITZBANKS. Gloria patria et filio et spiritui sancto;
        Sicut erat in principio et nunc et semper et in saecula saeculorum.

FORTESCUE *waits for a moment longer here, then lunges at the asparagus tart, but* FITZBANKS *still has not finished.*

FITZBANKS. Benedictus, Benedicat, Per Jesum
        Christum dominum nostrum.

   This time FORTESCUE *waits, head lowered, for the inevitable next line, whilst* FITZBANKS *and* DEBORAH *start eating.*

FITZBANKS. Tuck in Charles! You must be starving.

*S*ome time later. FORTESCUE *and* DEBORAH *are walking along an avenue of tall trees in the dying spring sunshine.*

DEBORAH. I've kept all your letters.

FORTESCUE. I kept yours.

DEBORAH. Yes ... They're all upstairs, in numbered boxes.

FORTESCUE. Oh, Deborah!

DEBORAH. The first eight boxes are general subjects.

FORTESCUE. Yes ...

DEBORAH. They're subdivided into specific sections.

FORTESCUE. Yes?

DEBORAH. And there are six for *particular* subjects ... birthdays, Christmas, Easter ... that sort of thing ...

FORTESCUE. Ah ...

DEBORAH. So I can find July 8th 1898, see 'Elephants' Box five ... Section three.

FORTESCUE. How busy you must have been!

DEBORAH. Oh, I enjoyed it. I *love* filing.

FORTESCUE *(gently)*. And ... where did you keep the letter in which I asked you to marry me?

DEBORAH *(confidently)*. Box three. Section eleven ...

FORTESCUE. Ah. *(He's silenced for a moment.)* ... I hope I didn't ... sound awfully forward ...

DEBORAH. No, not at all.

FORTESCUE. I mean, I did think about you an awful lot ...

DEBORAH. Well, I know – otherwise you wouldn't have written all those letters ...

FORTESCUE. Yes, you're right ...

DEBORAH. Six hundred and eighty-three.

FORTESCUE *(remembering, with a smile)*. Sitting out under the vast bowl of stars with all the sounds of the plain around me ...

DEBORAH. And a hundred and forty-three postcards.

FORTESCUE *(now miles away)*. One felt so awesomely tiny ... humble ...

DEBORAH. They wouldn't all fit in my room. I had to put 18B to 22S in the study and the odd numbers fifteen to twenty-one in Daddy's bedroom ... what I really want is one of the easy recall box-file systems with the spring-loaded spine control ...

Her voice fades.

*L*ater that evening FORTESCUE *is unpacking. He hums a hymn to himself as he takes out the dusty relics of ten years in Africa. He takes out a picture of Queen Victoria on which the glass has cracked. He tut-tuts. He takes out one of Edward VII and, blowing the sand off, he looks round for somewhere to put it. He sees a space on the mantelpiece, but he has to move one of the fertility symbols. He puts the picture down, then holds the fertility symbol for a moment. It is the same one with which he made such an impression on the elegant lady on the boat. His brow furrows as he looks down at it. The image of the lady during their brief encounter on the deck comes clearly into his mind. She is smiling at him. He goes towards her. She smiles. He goes up to her and she is gone. He frowns to himself at this disturbing memory.*

The next day FORTESCUE *and* DEBORAH *are cycling together through the leafy lanes and beechwoods.*

FORTESCUE. This is marvellous! It's like seeing it all for the first time. I had an old boneshaker out in Africa for a while ...

DEBORAH. Yes, you said so in letters 18, 36 and 49.

FORTESCUE. I used to ride round the province on it. The locals hadn't seen one before. They called me the Man on the Starving Horse ...

They laugh.

DEBORAH. How silly ...

FORTESCUE. You really ought to have come out to Africa, you know ...

DEBORAH. No ... I can't stand being dirty. I'm going to be a jolly happy English vicar's wife and have a big house and lots of children. That's all I want.

FORTESCUE. We'll have to see what I'm offered. The Bishop may want me to be a prison chaplain or something.

DEBORAH. Oh, I don't fancy that much!

FORTESCUE *laughs, but not with much conviction.*

DEBORAH. Oh, I can't wait to be married, Charles.

She passes him, FORTESCUE *cycles after her, looking thoughtful.*

London. Heart of the Empire. May 1906.

FORTESCUE *is making his way along crowded city streets. He keeps taking out a piece of paper and checking an address. Finally he stops and looks up; a discreet plaque on the side of a building reads 'The Church and Universities Club'. He is about to mount the imposing steps and enter when his eye is caught by something further down the street. Sure enough, emerging from a building some fifty yards away is the* ELEGANT LADY *in yet another magnificent outfit.*

FORTESCUE *stops dead.*

She crosses the pavement towards a waiting cab. FORTESCUE *takes a couple of steps towards her. As she reaches the cab she looks round. Straight at him.* FORTESCUE *opens his mouth as if to speak, when a well-dressed, prosperous middle-aged man steps out of the cab. He holds the door open for her and she gets in without another glance at* FORTESCUE, *who steps back in embarrassment and collides with two elderly gentlemen walking up the street. He turns, flushed, and hurries into the club, shaking his head. He trips up on the kerb, thus compounding his embarrassment. The* ELEGANT LADY *smiles as her brougham passes up the street.*

FORTESCUE *finds himself in a dark and inhospitable hallway with enormously high dusty ceilings. No one seems to be about;* FORTESCUE *ventures in. From the depths of the cavernous gloom an aged porter appears.*

FORTESCUE. Er. The Bishop of London?

Without a word, and without breaking his shuffle, the dust-covered old man points to some stairs.

FORTESCUE, *thanking him, walks up the hallway. He turns left at the end of the hallway and finds himself at the top of the stairs leading down. As he goes down he hears the unlikely sound of a boxing bout, punctuated by the occasional shouted instruction and exhortation. The sounds get louder, and he finds himself at the doors to a gallery overlooking the gymnasium. He pushes open the door.*

A long gymnasium in which a dozen or so young men are training at press-ups, Indian clubs, wall-bars, wrestling. A small group of spectators are clustered around, a couple of young first-year undergraduates boxing. Outside the ring sit two other boxers, a coach in university colours, and a sharp, fit, lean man in early middle age with dog collar and Bishop's purple, an Oxford college sweater, long shorts and gym shoes. He watches the boys keenly. He it is who first looks up as the door shuts behind FORTESCUE.

BISHOP. Fortescue!

Heads turn at this celebrated name, including momentarily the head of one of the boxers, who receives a cracking blow on the ear.

BISHOP *(bounding up from his chair with surprising agility).* Come down!

FORTESCUE *enters the gym and the* BISHOP *approaches him, arm outstretched. They shake hands.*

BISHOP. Sorry to drag you down here but it's my Young Men's night. Can't miss it. Like a scrap?

FORTESCUE. I'm sorry?

BISHOP *(nodding at the ring).* I love to see a pair of fit boys scrapping . . .

A bloodstained face thuds against one of the canvas uprights beside them.

He studies the ring approvingly for a moment, then suddenly rounds on the somewhat confused FORTESCUE *again.*

BISHOP. Hockey?

FORTESCUE. What?

BISHOP. Play hockey?

FORTESCUE. Not really, no, my Lord.

BISHOP. Oh, too bad. Promised I'd get a team together to play the Methodists – Saturday week. They're very good. But physical. Worried. Drink?

FORTESCUE. A cup of tea would be nice . . .

BISHOP. Tea it shall be. Wise man . . . *(He bounds across to a serving hatch and raps on the counter.)* Two of your finest, please, Hilda. Well . . . how was Africa . . . ?

FORTESCUE. Oh . . . quite remarkable.

BISHOP. Much time for sport?

FORTESCUE. Er . . . No, not really.

BISHOP. I was out there for a bit you know. Amazing country. Tried to organise some rugby football but it really wasn't their sort of thing. They hold on to the ball for too long . . . weeks sometimes.

Two cups are plonked messily on to the counter.

BISHOP *(to the ring).* Keep your arms up Leggit! *(Then he returns to* FORTESCUE*).* They don't like rules, that's the trouble. We had a chap called Sperry in Tabaka province. Keen cricketer . . . county standard. Tried to explain the no-ball rule to a very primitive side from Mashonaland. They cut his head off in the tea interval. Stuck it on the pavilion . . .

FORTESCUE. Oh dear God . . .

BISHOP. Worst thing was, he'd built that pavilion himself . . . Still . . . just shows. Can't force the pace of progress . . . Well, cheers. *(He stirs vigorously and taps the spoon carefully on the side of the cup.)* Well, let me get straight to the reason why I brought you back, Fortescue. *(He takes a loud and elaborate drink of tea, lowers his cup and takes one final look around.)* How are you with women?

FORTESCUE *(very startled)*. I beg your pardon, sir.

BISHOP. I know you're good with Africans, but how are you with women?

FORTESCUE. I'm sorry. I'm not quite sure what you mean, sir.

BISHOP. They are a problem, Fortescue . . . an increasing problem . . .

FORTESCUE. Women?

BISHOP. Certain kinds of women, yes . . .

FORTESCUE *(cautiously)*. Certain kinds . . .

BISHOP *(leaning across confidentially)*. Ladies of the street, *filles de joie*. Big problem for the Church. We're strong on drunkenness, we've had a fair crack at homelessness, but as far as prostitution goes, we're not even out of the changing room.

FORTESCUE. What do you want *me* to do, my Lord?

BISHOP. Go amongst prostitutes, Fortescue. Go into the filthiest streets of London, into the back alleys and behind the workhouses and seek out the harlots and the streetwalkers . . .

A bead or two of perspiration has broken out on FORTESCUE's *forehead.*

BISHOP. . . . get to know them . . . get to understand them . . . win their confidence. Find out why they do what they do . . . and stop them doing it.

The TRAINER *comes across to the* BISHOP.

TRAINER. Sir, sorry to bother you, but he's knocked him out . . . Broken his nose, sir.

BISHOP. Good. Give him a rest. Then try him on that young chap – Greenidge.

TRAINER. Right, sir.

BISHOP. We desperately need this Mission, Fortescue. Your Methodist, your Salvationist, even your Catholic, is showing us the way home. We're starting a lap behind, but we can still get our nose ahead at the bell . . . What d'you say?

FORTESCUE. I don't know what to say . . . It's not really what I had . . . er . . . expected.

BISHOP. No, I realise it's a difficult one to bowl at you, just out of the blue like that . . . All I would ask is that you come dancing with me tonight.

FORTESCUE *looks up in amazement.*

That same evening FORTESCUE *and the* BISHOP *find themselves in a small noisy East End dance hall. On the stage a singer is belting out the evergreen Cockney ballad, 'Put on Yer Ta-Ta Little Girlie'. No one is listening. There is a crush of people meeting, talking and drinking.*

FORTESCUE *looks wide-eyed, the* BISHOP *stern. He stops and points grimly ahead. At a dark corner of the bar numerous girls are offering themselves to the punters for money. There are girls on old men's knees, or draped round half-cupped customers. One or two men are handing over money.*

The BISHOP's *face creases in disgust.*

BISHOP *(shouting back at* FORTESCUE *over the noise).* You see the scale of the problem?

FORTESCUE *is caught rather off-guard, looking round at all this willing flesh with more curiosity than disapproval.*

FORTESCUE. Yes . . . yes . . . I do . . . But I really think I should be getting back . . . they're expecting me at a fund-raising concert. I'm to be the guest of honour . . .

BISHOP. There's worse than this . . . Come on!

Meanwhile, back in Oxfordshire, in the library of Lord and Lady Fermleigh's baronial hall, a string quartet are playing a piece of Beethoven. They aren't obviously bad, and indeed our first impression is of rather pleasing melodiousness. But on closer examination it's clear that they aren't very well in time. Only the occasional swift glance of mutual disapproval from CELLIST to LEAD VIOLIN betrays their awareness that anything is wrong. They are immaculately dressed in tails and white tie and gloves.

After a few moments we cut to the audience. In the front row of the audience LADY FERMLEIGH smiles beatifically up at the quartet. The REVEREND FITZBANKS and DEBORAH sit beside her and beside them sits a sea of empty chairs. In all there are about eighteen dinner-jacketed guests, including the inevitable couple of clergymen, in rows of seats set out for about a hundred. At the back at least fifteen servants stand waiting behind a table piled with sandwiches and soft drinks. On the front of the tablecloth we read 'Winter Clothes for the Zulus Evening'. In the back row by the door sits the ELEGANT LADY with a fashionable young man in tow. She, like DEBORAH, is not entirely concentrating on the music, aware as they both are, of someone's absence. The music gets worse. LADY FERMLEIGH, still smiling beatifically, leans across to DEBORAH.

LADY FERMLEIGH. Beautiful . . . isn't it . . .

Meanwhile, back in the seedy dance-hall, a hapless but fascinated FORTESCUE is being dragged by the BISHOP through the bar, attracting a few wolf-whistles and propositions from the naughty ladies . . .

BISHOP. Look at them . . . some are only thirteen, fourteen . . .

The BISHOP pushes up to the bar and approaches a startled girl. She is hardly into her teens.

BISHOP. How old are you, my dear?

VERY YOUNG PROSTITUTE. Twenty-three.

BISHOP (only momentarily lost for words). You don't have to do this work, you know . . .

VERY YOUNG PROSTITUTE. Go away!

A sinister long-haired man approaches. His name is ARTHUR PIMP.

PIMP. Come on, gents. One at a time.

BISHOP. I am a bishop.

PIMP. Sorry, sir . . . there's no reductions.

The PROSTITUTE *briefly catches* FORTESCUE's *eye. He stares at her young, over-made-up face, with fascinated horror.*

BISHOP. I can help you find other work . . .

PIMP. Come on!

BISHOP *(brushing* MR PIMP's *hand off his arm)*. Come back with us. We'll see you're fed and clothed. You won't have to come back to all this degradation.

PIMP *(shouts)*. Harry! Trouble . . .

BISHOP. Come on . . . Come with us . . .

VERY YOUNG PROSTITUTE. Get off!

The girl screams, as out of the shadows two men leap on FORTESCUE *and the* BISHOP. *The barman leaps over to separate the fighters. Girls scream, other men join in on either side, and a full-scale brawl develops; a chair is hurled, it flies right past the bar and removes the singer from the stage in mid-chorus. Scream as he crashes into the audience.*

Back at the 'Winter Clothes for the Zulus Evening', the quartet are murdering Handel.

LADY FERMLEIGH. Isn't it lovely?

FITZBANKS. Absolutely delightful, Lady Fermleigh. A most successful concert.

LADY FERMLEIGH *(nodding at the orchestra)*. All slightly handicapped, you know.

FITZBANKS. Well, I think it's marvellous what you do for them.

LADY FERMLEIGH. Oh, yes. The only things they can't cope with are the guns.

FITZBANKS *(nonplussed)*. The guns?

LADY FERMLEIGH. At the end . . . when they fire the guns in the middle of the music . . . These smaller orchestras can't afford the weapons . . .

FITZBANKS. Ah . . . that's the 1812 . . . Tchaikovsky.

But LADY FERMLEIGH *isn't listening. She leans across to* DEBORAH *with a benign smile.*

LADY FERMLEIGH. I'm so sorry about our guest of honour . . . I did so want to meet him.

DEBORAH. I'm frightfully sorry. I can't think what's kept him.

LADY FERMLEIGH. Oh, I'm sure he's a very busy man. He was in India, wasn't he?

DEBORAH. Africa.

LADY FERMLEIGH. Ah, yes. My husband was in Japan.

It is the next morning. DEBORAH *is working at the beehives with the help of* PARSWELL, *who wears an improvised beekeeper's net which makes him look not unlike the Grand Wizard of the Klu Klux Klan.* DEBORAH *raises her veil as* FORTESCUE's *coach rattles up the drive to the front door.* MAJOR *opens one bloodshot eye.* FORTESCUE *jumps out, pays the driver and turns towards the house. His face is bruised and he has traces of a bloodied nose but his eyes shine with an inner light of crusading determination. He grins at* MAJOR *and bends to pat him fondly.* MAJOR *leaps away from* FORTESCUE's *touch and barks surlily at him from a distance.*

DEBORAH *appears at the door, looking anxious.*

DEBORAH. Oh, Charles, we were so worried about you. Are you all right?

FORTESCUE. Yes, I'm absolutely fine . . .

DEBORAH. Oh, thank goodness! I had visions of you getting into all sorts of trouble. What happened to your poor head?

FORTESCUE. Oh, that's nothing . . . I banged it . . . on the door . . . of the train . . . er . . . *(Brightly.)* How was the concert?

DEBORAH. *Everyone* was asking after you. They're all terribly excited about the wedding . . .

FORTESCUE. The wedding?

DEBORAH. *Our* wedding . . .

FORTESCUE. Ah yes . . .

He walks into the rectory. DEBORAH *follows.*

DEBORAH. Well, don't be so mysterious, do tell me . . .

EMILY *steps forward to take* FORTESCUE's *coat . . .*

DEBORAH. Is it an *important* job?

FORTESCUE *(slipping out of his coat)*. Yes . . . Yes, it is an important job, Deborah.

> *He fixes her with an intense stare which makes her a little uncomfortable.*

FORTESCUE. . . . Desperately important . . .

> FORTESCUE *walks through into the dining-room.* DEBORAH *follows in excited anticipation.*

FORTESCUE *(as he walks)*. It's . . . not exactly what I'd expected . . . But, by God, it needs doing and I shall do it the best I possibly can!

EMILY *(softly)*. Something hot, sir? *(She indicates the remains of breakfast on a hot-plate.)*

FORTESCUE. Rather! *(He helps himself liberally to kedgeree and walks to the table.)*

DEBORAH. Well, what is it?

FORTESCUE *(eyes staring with excitement)*. I'm going to remain a missionary.

DEBORAH *(her face falls)*. But I thought . . .

FORTESCUE. A missionary *in* England . . .

DEBORAH. But everyone's English in England.

FORTESCUE. Yes, but that doesn't mean that they are any less needful of our help. *(He turns to her.)* Deborah, I saw things last night which will never leave my memory. In the heart of our capital city, in the centre of our Empire, I saw people who have no home but the street . . .

DEBORAH. You mean tramps?

FORTESCUE. Yes, tramps *and* others . . .

DEBORAH *(with scarce-concealed disappointment)*. Are you going to help *tramps*?

FORTESCUE *(he breathes deeply)*. I'm going to be helping women.

DEBORAH. Women *tramps*?

FORTESCUE. Well no . . . Women who are in . . . er . . . in moral trouble.

DEBORAH. Liars?

> FORTESCUE *stops. A profound weariness spreads over his face. He turns to* DEBORAH. *He goes to take her by the shoulders. She moves out of his reach rather smartly.*

DEBORAH *(shocked)*. Not yet, Charles!

> *He controls himself and glances at* EMILY *who is quietly clearing away.* EMILY *nods and leaves . . .* FORTESCUE *indicates a chair.*

FORTESCUE. Deborah . . . sit down . . .

> *He pulls out a chair and sits opposite her.*

FORTESCUE *(very seriously)*. I want to talk this over with you so we both know exactly what we are doing. The Mission is going to be a very large part of my life from now on.

DEBORAH. Milk?

FORTESCUE. Yes, please. I promised the Bishop I would not only run it but I would find the money to run it. This will take time and take me away from you. So I want you to be absolutely clear about what –

DEBORAH. Sugar?

FORTESCUE *(with faint irritation)*. Two – yes . . . About what I'm taking on . . . Deborah, do you know what is meant by 'fallen women'?

DEBORAH. Women who've hurt their knees?

FORTESCUE. No . . . no . . . much worse than that.

DEBORAH. Broken their legs?

FORTESCUE. Oh dear . . .

NARRATOR: Only slightly deterred by Deborah's evident inability fully to comprehend the nature of his work, Fortescue threw himself into the task of fund-raising with characteristic vigour.

Fermleigh Hall, *a few days later.*

A long, spacious living-room full of all sorts of old and rare objects, one of which is LORD FERMLEIGH, *a shrunken, aged little man who sits, almost lost in a huge chair, with a rug over his lower half. The door opens. Little* LADY FERMLEIGH *enters, leading* FORTESCUE *by the hand.*

LADY FERMLEIGH. Cedric dear . . . someone to see you . . .

LORD FERMLEIGH. Oh . . .

LADY FERMLEIGH. This is Mr Fortescue . . . the missionary! You remember we read all about him in the newspapers.

LORD FERMLEIGH. Oh?

LADY FERMLEIGH. He wants us to help him in his new work, dear. Isn't that splendid?

FORTESCUE *(approaching the old man's chair with his arm out).* How do you do, sir? I'm *so* pleased to meet you ...

LADY FERMLEIGH *(pleasantly).* Don't shake his hand ... it's a terrible palaver ...

FORTESCUE. Ah ... *(He addresses* LORD FERMLEIGH *politely.)* It's a most beautiful house ...

LADY FERMLEIGH. He won't hear that, I'm afraid ...

FORTESCUE *(louder).* It's a most beautiful house.

LORD FERMLEIGH. Mm?

LADY FERMLEIGH. No, he doesn't hear anything on that side ...

> She indicates the sofa opposite.

FORTESCUE. Oh, I see ... *(He crosses over.)* I was saying what a beautiful house you have here ...

LADY FERMLEIGH. No ... no ... that's *too* close ...

FORTESCUE *(backing away).* What a beautiful house this is!!

> LORD FERMLEIGH *looks up and smiles.*

LORD FERMLEIGH. Hello ...

LADY FERMLEIGH. There you see ... You've got him now ... it's all to do with a war wound – the Crimea, you know.

FORTESCUE. Well my feeling is, your lordship ... *(He comes close to him and sits.)* ... that after spending ten very fruitful years in Africa ... I realised that in all that time I've been neglecting the needs of our own people here at home ... *(He looks – no reaction;* LORD FERMLEIGH *remains huddled up under his rug.)* You see, it's all very well sending missions out to Indo-China and the Gambia and Somaliland ... when the real problems are here,

32

under our very noses. *This* is the country that needs help ... All our best people leave for Africa ... for the colonies ... and what do they leave behind them, here, on our doorstep?

Silence from LORD FERMLEIGH. LADY FERMLEIGH *smiles happily.*

FORTESCUE. A moral void ... At the hearts of our great cities ... In the back streets and behind the workhouses ... and in the slum tenements ...

FORTESCUE *warms to his theme and, carried away by his own oratory and conviction, turns his back on the* FERMLEIGHS *and walks towards the window, orating as if to an imaginary congregation.*

FORTESCUE. ... You will find in the middle of it all there are young women, some no more than eleven or twelve years old, who wander the streets, homeless, the prey of criminals and exploiters. They know no pride and no shame as they sink further into the abyss. I have seen them, I have talked to them and I have heard their cries for help ...

LADY FERMLEIGH *looks across to her husband, then looks again more closely, peering through her pince-nez.*

FORTESCUE. ... If society turns its head away now ... if we refuse to fight, refuse to help ... If we pass by on the other side then He will call us to account.

LADY FERMLEIGH *reaches discreetly for the bell-pull.*

FORTESCUE. ... He will want to know why it was that we left our own people in the mire and the filth of evil ... why we could see so clearly the mote in others' eyes but not the beam in our own. I tell you ...

A maid enters.

FORTESCUE. ... that unless we can take up the battle to save and enlighten these wretched souls, *now* ...

LADY FERMLEIGH *whispers briefly to the maid. The maid nods and goes out.*

FORTESCUE. ... Then we will find that the darkness of ignorance which we see so clearly in others will soon engulf us all, and we will become sucked into the quicksands of licentiousness and moral decay ...

A door opens. The maid shows in a doctor. But FORTESCUE *has his back to them.*

FORTESCUE. ... I feel most deeply that we cannot and must not take the easy way out – to ignore what is going on ... to think it will never affect us ...

The doctor crosses to LORD FERMLEIGH, *and gives him a quick examination.*

FORTESCUE. We *can* begin a moral revival, we *can* begin to save the souls of English women who have fallen into sin, those who have sold their minds and bodies to evil ...

The doctor goes to LADY FERMLEIGH. *A quick whispered consultation. They look over at* LORD FERMLEIGH.

FORTESCUE. ... but we must begin now, and it is why I am here today, because ...

LADY FERMLEIGH *raises her hand to interrupt.* FORTESCUE *is so carried away he doesn't notice.*

FORTESCUE. ... I believe that it is here that we can start a new and vigorous ...

LADY FERMLEIGH. Mr Fortescue ...

FORTESCUE. ... tide of hope and optimism!

LADY FERMLEIGH. Mr Fortescue ...

FORTESCUE. ... that will breach the walls of ignorance!

LADY FERMLEIGH (*getting up*). Mr Fortescue . . .

FORTESCUE. . . . and smash the barriers of . . . Yes?

LADY FERMLEIGH. I'm awfully sorry but my husband's died.

FORTESCUE. Died?

LADY FERMLEIGH. Yes, you know his heart has ceased to . . .

FORTESCUE. Yes, yes . . . I know what you . . . er . . . oh, dear . . .

He's covered in some confusion. A butler enters with a sheet. He and the doctor put it over the old man.

LADY FERMLEIGH. I am so terribly sorry, because he would have loved to have heard what you were saying . . .

FORTESCUE. No . . . no, I'm the one that should be sorry . . . I do apologise . . .

LADY FERMLEIGH. Oh, don't worry . . . these things happen, Mr Fortescue, and he's had a jolly good innings . . .

The doctor and the butler carry the old man out.

FORTESCUE. I'd better go, I'm so sorry . . .

LADY FERMLEIGH. No . . . no. *I'm* sorry. He's so forgetful. He probably forgot you were there.

FORTESCUE. Well, I think when one's dying, one does become, er . . . forgetful . . .

LADY FERMLEIGH (*quite distressed*). He's never done it before.

A day or two later and the indefatigable FORTESCUE *is with a large florid self-made man,* MR MCEVOY, *walking down between a line of rattling noisy machines operated by lines of grubby, sweating operatives.*

FORTESCUE. It's very good of you to see me on this matter, Mr McEvoy...

MCEVOY. Oh, it's a great privilege, Mr Fortescue... I've always admired the work you do in Africa – as does everyone in the company. I think people like ourselves should work together more closely. We are but two strong arms of the same great body of civilisation. You with your education and religion and us with our soft drinks.

FORTESCUE. Well, I might as well make myself clear from the start... I am here to appeal to your generosity, Mr McEvoy...

MCEVOY. Well, you couldn't have found a more generous man, though I say it myself, Fortescue. I come from a long line of generous people. My grandfather, whose portrait hangs over our safe, was the personification of the charitable act... the McEvoy Workhouses... the McEvoy Buildings... and the McEvoy Trust – all sadly inoperative now...

FORTESCUE. Oh dear...

MCEVOY. Yes... he was over-generous I'm afraid. But his spirit lives on in this firm – believe you me...

FORTESCUE. Well, that's what I'd hoped. You see, much of the work I shall be doing is not popular amongst those who endow our great charities...

MCEVOY. Because they have no vision. They're little men, making little decisions. They cannot see that money spent now is an investment for the future...

FORTESCUE. I'm so glad to hear you say that . . .

MCEVOY. Oh, yes . . . Africa is going to explode in the next ten or fifteen years . . . we're only seeing the tip of the iceberg. We sold our first bottle of McEvoy's 'Yellow Whippet' Lemon Tonic in southern Africa twelve years ago, now we're shipping a thousand crates a week to Zanzibar, Durban and Mozambique.

FORTESCUE. Ah, but . . .

MCEVOY. No, I know what you're going to say . . . that I'm just a mercenary businessman, but no . . . The missionary in Africa is an absolutely equal partner. You try selling lemonade to non-Christians . . .

FORTESCUE. Well, this is all very good to hear but . . .

MCEVOY. So what is it? A schoolroom – a mission house, irrigation scheme . . . ?

FORTESCUE. But I'm not working in Africa any more.

MCEVOY *(suddenly interested)*. Borneo? Burma?

FORTESCUE. No . . . London . . .

MCEVOY *(stopping and turning on* FORTESCUE*)*. London?

FORTESCUE. Yes, that's right.

MCEVOY. London – England?

FORTESCUE. Yes, I've been asked on behalf of the Church Missionary Society to open a new mission for Fallen Women . . .

MCEVOY. Fallen Women . . . ?

FORTESCUE. Women of the streets, *filles de joie* . . .

MCEVOY. *Prostitutes . . . ?*

FORTESCUE. Yes, that's right . . . And we will be needing a mission house, and possibly a schoolroom certainly . . .

MCEVOY. Ah. Well . . . we already have plenty of outlets in London . . .

FORTESCUE. I see.

MCEVOY (walking to a door). Oh yes, we don't need any more in London . . . We sell all we produce here. (A voice calls out to him.) Yes! I'm coming.

FORTESCUE. I see . . . and you're not interested in helping out with perhaps just one . . .

MCEVOY. I'm sorry, I couldn't persuade my board, Mr Fortescue. (He pulls open a door and smiles humourlessly.) Prostitutes are a very small part of our market. (Over the noise of the loading bay.) Find your own way out, can you?

The door slides shut behind FORTESCUE. MCEVOY talks to his foreman.

MCEVOY. What is it?

FOREMAN. Where do we put this ammonic acid?

MCEVOY. In the lemonade! Where the hell do you think you put it?

FOREMAN. It's poisonous . . .

MCEVOY. It's not very poisonous . . .

FOREMAN (doubtful). Well . . .

MCEVOY. How many bottles of that lemonade would you have to drink to kill yourself?

FOREMAN. . . . About two hundred . . .

MCEVOY. Well, there you are . . . Bloody Sambos probably use it for washing in anyway. They don't know one end of a bottle from another out there . . .

*B*ack at the rectory, FORTESCUE walks wearily into the hall. He crosses to the fireplace and stands staring gloomily into the fire a moment. He shakes his head as a door clicks. He looks up. It's EMILY, looking prettier than ever in the flickering firelight.

EMILY. Take your coat, sir?

FORTESCUE (smiling as best he can). Thank you, Emily.

She slips his coat off gently. This sudden moment of intimacy is shattered by DEBORAH's jolly voice calling from upstairs.

DEBORAH. Charles!

Something to do with the mindless cheeriness of her tone causes FORTESCUE to react with a most un-Christian grimace.

FORTESCUE. Yes, what is it?

DEBORAH. Come up here, I've got a surprise for you! In my bedroom!

FORTESCUE reacts in surprise at this, but leaves the fireside, and walks upstairs with a look of curious apprehension. He approaches her room. The door is ajar. He knocks lightly.

DEBORAH. Door's open!

He pushes the door and enters. Whatever hint of forbidden pleasures may have been seeded in his mind is shattered by what he sees. Superimposed on to a once delicately furnished feminine bedroom is a veneer of complex stationery equipment. DEBORAH is surrounded by papers, letters, lists and filing cabinets. Shelves are full of FORTESCUE's letters, neatly labelled. DEBORAH herself is on her knees in the middle of it all. She looks up at him, smiling, and looking very pleased with herself.

DEBORAH. Look in 'Incoming' *(She indicates a section of sorting office style shelving.)* under 'A'...

FORTESCUE *picks out a letter and reads ... He looks up, puzzled.*

FORTESCUE. Who is this Lady Ames?

DEBORAH. *Lord* Ames' wife ...!

FORTESCUE. Who?

DEBORAH. Lord Ames? Where have you been for the last ten years, Darkest Africa? Oh. *(She snorts apologetically.)* Well, he's frightfully important. He was General Gordon's number two.

FORTESCUE. Yes, but why does she want to give me his money all of a sudden? I didn't write to her.

DEBORAH. Of course you didn't, silly ... *I* wrote to her. According to the books he's the richest man in Britain. I thought it was worth starting there ...

FORTESCUE *looks down again at the letter, then slowly at* DEBORAH. *His face breaks into an affectionate smile. He goes towards her.*

FORTESCUE. Deborah ... *(He leans down towards her.)* ... you are a very very clever girl ...

He makes to peck her on the cheek but she neatly avoids him, leaving him pursing his lips at mid air.

DEBORAH. I just want to get us married, that's all ...

Ⓐ *fashionable Chelsea portrait studio.*

LORD AMES *is set impressively in determined profile against a rather idealised watercolour backcloth of the Battle of Omdurman. He wears a splendid full dress uniform. He's talking while maintaining his dignified profile pose, and holding the reins of a splendid horse's head. It all adds up to a very fine sight, except that the horse he is sitting astride is no more than a rather rickety wooden frame. A bit like a children's rocking horse.*

LORD AMES *(addressing some invisible audience)*. I suppose I was right to wear the Hussars uniform rather than the Lancers. It goes rather well with my eyes.

AMES *speaks to* SIR CYRIL EVERIDGE, *a distinguished looking, white-haired academician quietly painting away. The studio reflects the opulence, respectability and status of his patrons.*

LORD AMES. Shows every drop of blood, though. And of course, spume. Equine spume plays havoc with a cavalry uniform. An over-excited mount can make the most splendidly attired officer look as if he's suffering from appalling diarrhoea.

FORTESCUE *is shown in by a footman. He stands hat in hand, looking rather confused.* AMES' *monologue is interrupted by the sharp click of the studio door shutting.* AMES *turns his head sternly and casts a dyspeptic eye in* FORTESCUE's *direction. Quick reaction of despair from the* ARTIST *as* AMES *moves yet again.*

AMES. Who's that fellow? No one I know . . .

A voice from behind FORTESCUE.

VOICE. No . . . it's someone I know . . .

FORTESCUE *turns. There sitting towards the back of the studio, looking up from an expensive soft furnishings catalogue, is the* ELEGANT LADY *from the boat.* FORTESCUE *looks in some confusion from one to the other . . . She sets down her book, and with a wondrous smile stands and advances on* FORTESCUE, *hand outstretched.*

LADY AMES. I'm Lady Ames . . . I'm so glad you could come . . .

They shake hands.

LORD AMES. Is he British?

SIR CYRIL EVERIDGE. Your Lordship!

LORD AMES. Sorry . . . sorry . . . *(He turns his head into profile again.)* I find that as the years go on, I hate foreigners more and more. D'you find that, Everidge?

We leave AMES *rambling on and follow* LADY AMES *and* FORTESCUE.

LADY AMES *(to* FORTESCUE*)*. My husband's rather busy at the moment . . . Shall we talk?

FORTESCUE *(confused, pleased and quite lost for words)*. Er . . . Yes . . . yes of course . . .

She leads him to a conservatory at the back of the studio.

They sit at an alcove window seat. FORTESCUE *is rather tongue-tied by her dashing presence.*

LADY AMES. So . . . your fertility symbols arrived home safely . . .

FORTESCUE. Yes . . . a little bruised, perhaps . . . but . . .

LADY AMES. Effective none the less . . .

FORTESCUE *reddens and laughs nervously.*

LADY AMES. You must find it all very different here from Africa . . .

FORTESCUE. Yes . . . yes . . . it's a lot more civilised.

LADY AMES. Mm . . . that's the trouble, isn't it?

FORTESCUE. Trouble?

    LADY AMES *looks out of the window with a world-weary sweep of the arm.*

LADY AMES. Being civilised. I mean, here there are so many right ways of doing things and so many wrong ways of doing things . . .

FORTESCUE. It's the same in Africa, you know . . .

LADY AMES. Oh, I'm not talking about stealing cattle . . . I'm talking about what you're allowed to say and do . . .

FORTESCUE. Oh, England's very liberal after Africa . . . I assure you . . .

LADY AMES. D'you *really* think so? I find it very stifling . . .

    FORTESCUE *narrows his eyes. He can't make this woman out.*

FORTESCUE. . . . In what sort of way?

LADY AMES. Well . . . I mean, for instance, I couldn't just go around saying that I find you very attractive, could I?

    FORTESCUE *laughs nervously, glances quickly over towards* LORD AMES.

LADY AMES. It's all right . . . he's a talker, not a listener . . . Well . . . what do you think?

FORTESCUE *(carefully)*. Well, I think it's very kind of you to offer to donate money to the Mission . . . there is a very genuine need . . .

LADY AMES. About *me* . . .

FORTESCUE. About you . . . ? Well, as I say, I think you're extremely generous . . .

LADY AMES. Oh I am.

    She sees that FORTESCUE *is becoming uncomfortable with her playfulness.*

LADY AMES. Tell me about Africa . . .

FORTESCUE. Well, it's a very long story. Er . . . when I first went out in 'ninety-five . . .

LADY AMES. Does the sun shine all the time?

FORTESCUE *(smiling)*. Most of the time . . .

LADY AMES. I should like that . . .

FORTESCUE. Yes . . . it is very nice, once you get used to the flies and the fevers . . . Actually, it's tremendous. I loved it there . . . the people . . . And of course the animals . . . To wake up in the morning and see giraffe and hartebeeste and rhinos at the riverside . . .

LADY AMES. Why ever did you come back?

FORTESCUE. Oh, well, I didn't intend to stay there all my life . . . I wanted to come back. I wanted to try a new challenge. I wanted to . . .

LADY AMES. Be married?

FORTESCUE *(quickly)*. Yes . . . yes . . . Africa is all very well for a while, but it's not, er . . .

LADY AMES. Not what?

FORTESCUE. Well, it's not what . . . *(A little lamely.)* I was educated for . . . I mean my roots are here in England . . . like yours . . . *(This last without much conviction.)*

LADY AMES. Oh, my roots . . . yes . . . *(She sighs.)*

FORTESCUE. Well . . .

> FORTESCUE *pauses. He doesn't seem to know what to say. There is a charged atmosphere as they sit there. She stares at him, then looks away out of the window.*

FORTESCUE *(eventually)*. Did you want to discuss the donation with your husband . . . er . . .

LADY AMES. No . . . no . . . you're quite right. It's difficult to discuss it while he's here . . .

FORTESCUE. Er . . . no . . . that's not what I meant.

LORD AMES *(calls imperiously from the other end of the room)*. Isabel!

LADY AMES (*quickly*). Why don't you come and see me tomorrow, I have a bolthole in Chelsea. Here's the address.

She scribbles a number on a piece of paper and hands it to him.

LORD AMES. Isabel!

LADY AMES. Henry will be at the studio all day so we can just talk . . .

FORTESCUE (*hoarsely*). What?

LADY AMES. Get to know each other . . .

She gets up.

LADY AMES. David?

A footman comes over with FORTESCUE's *hat.*

LORD AMES (*impatiently*). Isabel!

LADY AMES (*equally impatiently*). Yes?

LORD AMES. Who are the people I *really* hate?

The doorman hands FORTESCUE *his hat and shows him to the door* . . .

LADY AMES (*as he passes her*). Please come . . . I think we could help each other . . .

FORTESCUE. Look, I'd rather we met . . .

LADY AMES. See you tomorrow. (*To* LORD AMES.) The Swiss?

FORTESCUE *is shown out, protesting vainly and soundlessly.*

LORD AMES. No . . . no . . . in *this* country . . . Who do I really hate? We were talking about them the other day . . .

LADY AMES (*glancing out of the window at Fortescue in the street below*). Missionaries.

LORD AMES (*vehemently*). That's right! Missionaries!

*T*he next day, at the rectory, EMILY the maid picks up a bowl of new potatoes and then takes them to the table, at which sits FITZBANKS, DEBORAH and a very thoughtful, anxiously silent FORTESCUE. EMILY leans close to FORTESCUE as she sets down the potatoes. He finds himself staring at EMILY's body, absently.

EMILY. Potatoes, sir . . .

FORTESCUE (*breaking out of his reverie*). No . . . no, thank you.

She offers them to FITZBANKS.

FITZBANKS (*helping himself liberally*). Thank you, Emily . . . any more halibut?

EMILY. No, sir . . . I'm afraid not, sir.

FITZBANKS. They were rather small halibut, were they not?

EMILY. Normal size, I think, sir.

FITZBANKS. And what is the normal size of a halibut, Emily?

EMILY. About eight inches, sir.

FITZBANKS. Really? As little as that.

EMILY *offers the bowl to* FORTESCUE.

FORTESCUE. No ... thank you.

He looks away and catches DEBORAH's *eye across the table.*

DEBORAH. Was he nice ... ?

FORTESCUE *doesn't react. He's drifted away again.*

DEBORAH. And *Lady* Ames. Was *she* nice?

FORTESCUE. Oh, yes ... yes ...

DEBORAH. Did she offer you anything?

FORTESCUE *(quickly)*. Er ... well ... she sort of hinted that she might be interested at some stage ...

DEBORAH. Then that's marvellous ...

EMILY *offers the potatoes again to* FITZBANKS *who again helps himself liberally.*

FITZBANKS. Very good people to be in with – Ames! Add a great deal of prestige ... open a few doors –

FORTESCUE. Well, I said 'no'.

DEBORAH. What?

FORTESCUE. I said 'no' ...

DEBORAH. You turned her *down*?

FORTESCUE. Yes ...

DEBORAH. Just like that ... without even thinking about it. You just said 'no' ...

FORTESCUE. I'm sorry ... I just didn't feel it was right ... I felt she was doing it for the wrong reasons ...

A rather stunned pause. FORTESCUE *takes more potatoes.*

FITZBANKS. Wouldn't have thought Ames was the sort of patron to turn down.

DEBORAH. But that's so rude . . . what must she think of you?

FORTESCUE. I'm sure I shall find the money elsewhere . . .

DEBORAH. That's what you've been saying for the last six weeks.

FORTESCUE. Please understand . . .

DEBORAH *(becoming tearful)*. No, I can't understand. First you tell me you're going to work with lady tramps, then you tell me that you've turned down the first real offer of money you've had . . . we're never going to get married . . . never!

She rushes out in tears.

FORTESCUE *(getting up)*. Deborah . . . Deborah, let me just explain . . .

He dashes out after her, banging his leg quite severely on the table in the process.

FITZBANKS. Well, I don't think she'll want her halibut . . .

He reaches across to DEBORAH's *plate and helps himself to it.*

DEBORAH *runs across the hall and into her father's study. The book-lined room is full of odd gadgets and a huge number of stuffed and semi-stuffed otters.* DEBORAH *is sobbing when* FORTESCUE *comes in.*

FORTESCUE. Deborah . . .

DEBORAH *(between sobs)*. I've waited ten years for you, Charles . . .

FORTESCUE. You must trust me, Deborah . . . There were reasons why I couldn't accept . . .

DEBORAH. What reasons?

FORTESCUE *(taking a deep breath)*. Er . . . just reasons . . .

DEBORAH. You're so mysterious about everything these days . . .

FORTESCUE *(impatiently)*. Look . . . what d'you want me to do!

DEBORAH *(recovering; dabbing at her eyes)*. Go and see her again, Charles.

FORTESCUE. I can't, I don't know where she'll be.

DEBORAH. Go to the studio.

FORTESCUE. They've finished now.

DEBORAH. Go to her house.

FORTESCUE *(quickly)*. I don't know where it is.

DEBORAH *(between the sobs)*. Moretonhampstead! It's on the Great Western line, two stops before Chippenham. There's a 9.38, a 12.06 and a 2.15.

FORTESCUE. Deborah, you don't understand . . .

DEBORAH *(suddenly determined)*. Please, Charles, if you love me, go back and see her . . .

FORTESCUE's *face shows a mixture of alarm and desperation. He closes his eyes.*

*T*he huge, impressive gates of Moretonhampstead House. FORTESCUE's anxious face appears between the bold curlicues. He stops and looks toward the house. It is enormous. He is wearing his Sunday best, and he carries a briefcase. He looks not unlike a travelling salesman. He pauses for a moment, runs his tongue over dry lips, then with a short nervous cough and a deep breath he walks boldly up the drive. After a quarter of a mile walk beside fountains and tended lawns, FORTESCUE reaches the door . . . there is no turning back now . . .

FORTESCUE pulls on the front door bell. A pause. In the deepest recesses of the house something stirs and presently the door is opened by a butler, SLATTERTHWAITE.

45

SLATTERTHWAITE. Yes?

FORTESCUE *(his voice faltering for a second)*. I . . . er . . . I believe the Ames' live here.

SLATTERTHWAITE. Yes.

FORTESCUE. Well . . . I would like to see Lady Ames. *(Adding quickly and firmly.)* On a purely business matter.

SLATTERTHWAITE. Of course, sir . . . Come this way please . . .

    FORTESCUE, *relieved to have got thus far, enters.* SLATTERTHWAITE *closes the mighty oak door behind them with a sonorous clang.*

SLATTERTHWAITE. Follow me please . . .

SLATTERTHWAITE *walks slowly and purposefully off across the hall.* FORTESCUE *falls in behind him.* SLATTERTHWAITE *is implacable,* FORTESCUE *still very unsure and tense. No sound save for their footsteps ringing out on marble floors. They round corners and pass through seemingly endless doorways. Finally* SLATTERTHWAITE *stops. They are in a small cloak-room, surrounded by guns, boots, coats, tennis rackets and hats.*

SLATTERTHWAITE. Mmm . . . no this can't be right. Should have turned left instead of right at the billiard room I think.

He turns and walks purposefully out.

SLATTERTHWAITE. This way, please, sir.

Again, SLATTERTHWAITE *leads impressively and* FORTESCUE *hurries along behind.* SLATTERTHWAITE *opens a door. Inside is a long thin room full of cheese on shelves and hanging from the ceiling.*

SLATTERTHWAITE. No, that's not it. *(He shuts the door and walks on.)*

FORTESCUE *(helpfully, as he follows on).* It *is* a very large house . . .

SLATTERTHWAITE. Yes, that certainly doesn't help. Ah – *(He turns towards a door at the end of a passageway.)* . . . this looks promising.

SLATTERTHWAITE *opens the door. They step out into daylight. They're standing in a small herb garden at the back of the house.*

SLATTERTHWAITE *(looking around).* I think if you won't mind sir, we'd better walk round to the front door and start again. I'm much better outside . . . This way please.

SLATTERTHWAITE *strides off to the left.* FORTESCUE *gestures to the right.* SLATTERTHWAITE *gives a quick 'Tut!' and a shake of the head.*

SLATTERTHWAITE. Of course, you're absolutely right.

SLATTERTHWAITE *leads* FORTESCUE *off to the right.*

Meanwhile, in the huge front room of the house, full of portraits of Lord Ames in various uniforms, LADY AMES, *looking rather more restrained than at the studio, is idly flicking through a society magazine as she walks. At a bureau,* LORD AMES *is writing a letter.*

LORD AMES. Are there two 'l's' in 'disembowelment'?

LADY AMES *(distantly)*. I think so . . .

She stops at the window . . .

LADY AMES *(with sudden interest)*. Are you expecting anyone?

LORD AMES. No! Thank God . . .

LADY AMES. I saw Slatterthwaite with someone in tow, going down by the pond.

As if this sort of thing happens quite regularly, LADY AMES *reaches for the bell pull beside the fireplace.*

LORD AMES *(without looking up)*. He is the most disastrous butler. Can't we get rid of him?

LADY AMES. Of course we can't. He's been here twenty-five years.

LORD AMES. I don't know why we ever got rid of Margerison.

LADY AMES. You know perfectly well why we got rid of Margerison.

LORD AMES. It was only a bit of harmless fun.

LADY AMES. Not to the parents.

MILLICENT, *the parlour maid, enters.*

MILLICENT. Yes, m'lady?

LADY AMES. Would you go and help find Mr Slatterthwaite, please Millicent? He's down by the rockery. Head him off before he gets to the maze.

MILLICENT. Yes, m'lady.

She curtsies and exits ... Silence. LADY AMES, *who is clearly bored, walks across the room. She absently riffles through a copy of the 'Illustrated London News', stares out of the window, then slides down on to the sofa crossing her long elegant legs. She stares unlovingly at her husband's back as he works at his desk.*

LADY AMES *(after a pause)*. What are you doing?

LORD AMES. Writing to *The Times* ...

LADY AMES *(not really interested)*. What about?

LORD AMES. Punishment.

LADY AMES. Ah ...

Pause ... *She flicks another page.*

LORD AMES. 'Embedded'?

LADY AMES. Two 'd's'.

LORD AMES. Thank you.

LORD AMES. 'Skull'?

LADY AMES *(sharply, irritably)*. S ... K ...

A knock sounds.

MILLICENT. The butler, Madam ...

LADY AMES. Thank you, Millicent.

There is quite a long pause, then SLATTERTHWAITE's *head, dishevelled and rather short of breath, peers round the door.*

SLATTERTHWAITE. Ah ... Lady ...?

LADY AMES *(helpfully)*. Ames ...

SLATTERTHWAITE. Lady Ames, a Mr Forrester to see you ...

LADY AMES *looks puzzled for a moment, then this turns to blank amazement as* FORTESCUE *enters. She flashes a look of recognition and warning at* FORTESCUE. *She looks across in alarm at her husband. But* FORTESCUE *has had plenty of time to rehearse and he swallows and leaps straight in . . .*

FORTESCUE *(extending a hand to* LORD AMES*)*. Good afternoon, sir. My name is Fortescue . . .

LADY AMES' *eyes widen further at this. Is the man mad?*

FORTESCUE. . . . I'm a missionary . . . I had the great good fortune of meeting you and your wife in London . . .

LORD AMES. Never seen you in my life . . .

FORTESCUE. At the studio, sir. You had most kindly offered some sympathetic support for my work.

LORD AMES. Most unlikely. What work is it?

FORTESCUE. Amongst the ... underprivileged, sir.

LORD AMES. Who?

FORTESCUE. The underprivileged, ...

LORD AMES. I'm not familiar with the term ...

FORTESCUE. People who have less than ourselves ...

LORD AMES. Ah ... well in our case that includes practically everyone in the country ... can you be more specific?

FORTESCUE. Yes ... I'm hoping to start a Mission ... er ... in the East End of London ...

LORD AMES. Well, that's totally out of the question.

FORTESCUE. Ah ...

LORD AMES. There's more harm been done in history by people trying to improve the lot of others than by all the wars and famines put together. Not a popular view but you'd be surprised by the number of terribly rich people who agree with me.

LADY AMES (looking at FORTESCUE with a mixture of relief and dawning admiration). Well, I certainly think we should know more about it ...

LORD AMES. Leave the ungrateful buggers alone, I say ...

LADY AMES. Won't you stay for dinner ...?

FORTESCUE. No, I have to get back to London this evening ... by nightfall ... (He adds unnecessarily.)

LADY AMES (raising an eyebrow). You've missed the last train.

FORTESCUE. I was told there was a 4.22.

LADY AMES (flashing a look). Not on Thursdays ...

FORTESCUE *(increasingly desperate)*. Coach?

LADY AMES. First thing in the morning . . .

LORD AMES. Can't Wooler get the car out?

LADY AMES. In *this* weather?

FORTESCUE. Look, I'll walk . . .

LADY AMES. You'll never make it.

> *She tugs at the bell pull and gives him a knowing conspiratorial smile.* FORTESCUE *smiles unhappily. Things are definitely getting out of control.*

LORD AMES. Can one *buy* a train?

LADY AMES. Where would we keep it . . .?

FORTESCUE. Look, why don't I come back –

> MILLICENT *enters.*

LADY AMES. Another one for dinner, Millicent.

MILLICENT. Yes, m'lady.

LADY AMES *(a definite hint of triumph in her husky voice)*. After all, it's not often we get missionaries in this part of Wiltshire . . .

With *a certain inevitability,* FORTESCUE *finds himself that evening in a splendid Adam dining-room. At the beautifully laid table, amidst cut glass and silver and candles sit the three of them.* FORTESCUE *on one side looking uncomfortable and still trying to avoid eye-contact with* LADY AMES *opposite. At the far end of the table, about a quarter of a mile away, sits* LORD AMES. *He leans across, picks up an exquisite wine decanter and pours himself a glass of white wine which shimmers and sparkles as it catches the candlelight.*

LORD AMES. You see, what I think is wrong with the country, today . . . is that there aren't enough people chained up . . .

> FORTESCUE *reacts.*

LADY AMES. It's one of his theories . . .

LORD AMES. I think many people, if they were given the choice between abject poverty and being held firmly, but fairly on a chain of their very own, would choose the chain . . . They could reach their food, obviously, lie down in bed, go for short walks –

LADY AMES *(impatiently)*. But you can't chain people up!

LORD AMES. Well, there you go you see – typical liberal reaction. All I'm saying is we should try it . . . see how it works . . . I tell you it would transform public order in this country overnight . . . Moselle?

FORTESCUE. No . . . thank you, I don't drink.

> *An exchange of looks.* LADY AMES *flashes him a smile he really doesn't need.*

LORD AMES. I've never tried to be popular, that's my strength. When I was in the army – the men used to call me 'Butcher Ames the Bastard Sadist' – but they loved me.

> *There is a click. The door opens and* SLATTERTHWAITE *enters, looking harassed, and carrying a magnificent soup tureen.*

SLATTERTHWAITE *(a little breathless as usual)*. Sorry I kept you waiting, sir . . . lost my bearings temporarily in the West Wing . . .

LORD AMES. I once had a chap before me who'd been caught stealing from the Mess. I had every alternate fingernail removed and, you know what, I still get a card from him every Christmas.

> SLATTERTHWAITE *serves a very cold soup . . .*

LADY AMES *(to FORTESCUE)*. Tired?

FORTESCUE. No . . . no . . . no, wide awake . . .

LADY AMES. You can go to bed whenever you want . . .

FORTESCUE. No . . . I really don't want you to go to any trouble . . .

LADY AMES. Trouble?

FORTESCUE. Well, of getting a room ready . . .

LADY AMES. We've got four hundred rooms ready, haven't we, Slatterthwaite?

SLATTERTHWAITE. At all times, my lady.

> *But he cannot cope with talking to* LADY AMES *and pouring* FORTESCUE'*s soup. In opting to talk to his mistress, he slowly and deliberately empties a ladle full of cream of asparagus down* FORTESCUE'*s shirt.*

FORTESCUE. Oh, I'm so sorry . . .

SLATTERTHWAITE *(realising)*. No, *I'm* sorry.

LADY AMES. D'you want to go up and change out of those wet things?

FORTESCUE *(quickly)*. No!

LADY AMES *(rising)*. But you're all sticky.

FORTESCUE. No, it's all right . . .

LADY AMES. You can't eat your dinner like that.

FORTESCUE. Well, I don't want any more dinner, I think I'll go to bed after all . . . I'm terribly tired all of a sudden . . .

LADY AMES. What a good idea. I'll send some food up.

FORTESCUE *(backing away)*. No, please don't. I mean, no, thank you.

LADY AMES. Millicent . . . the Chinese Room, please.

> SLATTERTHWAITE *is busy dabbing him down.* FORTESCUE *eases to the door.*

FORTESCUE. I am so sorry . . . what a mess . . . oh dear . . . good night . . .

> *He goes out. There is a short pause.*

LORD AMES. Has he been in Africa a long time?

LADY AMES. Ten years . . .

LORD AMES. Thought so . . . saw it in the Sudan. Bloody missionary – suddenly snapped . . . ate three tins of boot polish and ran stark naked into the church on Advent Sunday.

LADY AMES. Stark naked . . .?

LORD AMES. Not a stitch. Made straight for the choirboys.

> LADY AMES *glances at the door.*

> *A few moments later* FORTESCUE, *with the look of a man being led to the scaffold, is being shown into a well-appointed little bedroom by* MILLICENT, *the parlour maid. There is a vase of fresh flowers on the table, and the bed is turned back.* FORTESCUE *looks around suspiciously.*

56

MILLICENT. Here's your room, sir. There's a nightshirt for you sir on the bed . . . I hope you'll have everything you want tonight.

She curtsies and leaves, closing the door. FORTESCUE *goes quickly to the door and turns the key. He breathes a sigh of relief and turns back to the bed. The door opens behind him.*

MILLICENT. Oh, the locks don't work any more, sir. The mistress had them taken off . . .

She curtsies, smiles and goes out. FORTESCUE *nods his head resignedly.* MILLICENT's *footsteps disappear down the passage. He goes to the window, loosening his collar. He looks out. A perfect starlit summer night. The chestnut trees blow gently in the breeze. A church clock strikes distantly. The door opens. It's* SLATTERTHWAITE *carrying an enormous roast chicken on a dish.*

SLATTERTHWAITE *(seeing his mistake and going out as fast as he came in).* Sorry, sir! . . . Sorry!

Later *that same night.*

The room is bathed in the eerie glow of full moonlight. A chair is wedged underneath the handle. FORTESCUE *is asleep. There is a light knock at the door.*

FORTESCUE *sits bolt upright.*

FORTESCUE. Yes?

LADY AMES. Can I come in?

FORTESCUE. Er . . . what . . . for?

LADY AMES. We never did discuss how much you wanted – for the Mission . . .

FORTESCUE. Er . . . well it's rather late now . . .

LADY AMES. Yes, but I may not see you in the morning, I never get up frightfully early.

FORTESCUE. Oh . . . well er . . . yes . . . come in then . . . I'll get my . . . come in . . .

LADY AMES *rattles the door.*

FORTESCUE *(scrambling out of bed).* Just a moment . . . the chair fell against the door.

He gets out of bed, pulls a jacket over his nightshirt and moves the chair. He then darts back to a table and sets out some papers. LADY AMES *enters. She is in night-attire which causes him to look away nervously and make a grab for his clerical overcoat which he pulls on rather unsuccessfully.*

FORTESCUE *(trying to be busy).* Er . . . now . . . I have the papers here. I haven't got the exact figures . . . I wasn't expecting . . .

LADY AMES. You look rather good in Henry's nightshirt.

FORTESCUE *(taken aback).* Well, I'm very honoured to be wearing it.

LADY AMES. I often wondered what sort of things Henry wore in bed.

FORTESCUE. You . . . don't . . . ?

LADY AMES. God, no . . . that was never part of the arrangement. He only touches me by accident, in the car occasionally when we turn the corner too fast . . .

FORTESCUE *(embarrassed).* I'm sorry . . .

LADY AMES. Oh, there are others . . .

FORTESCUE *frowns.*

LADY AMES. Are you shocked?

FORTESCUE *shrugs uncomfortably*.

LADY AMES. You shouldn't be. Not if you're going to be any help to fallen women.

FORTESCUE *(delving in his briefcase)*. Yes, well, talking of fallen women, I think the first point should be the purchase of a suitable mortgage.

LADY AMES. How much do you want?

FORTESCUE *(eyes widening)*. Well, I think we should discuss it, don't you?

LADY AMES. No.

FORTESCUE. No...?

LADY AMES. Why pretend...?

FORTESCUE *(voice sinking)*. Pretend?

LADY AMES *(approaching, eyes blazing wilfully)*. I know why you came here today...

FORTESCUE *(backing away)*. If we could confine ourselves to the financial aspects, I think it would be better for both of us.

LADY AMES. You don't find me attractive?

FORTESCUE. No... it's not that.

LADY AMES. Why did you follow me in the street?

FORTESCUE. Follow you?

LADY AMES. In Pall Mall...

FORTESCUE. I wasn't following you.

LADY AMES. Why did you attack me on the boat?

FORTESCUE. *(helplessly)*. That was an accident!

LADY AMES. Why did you have your fiancée write to me?

FORTESCUE. Pure coincidence.

> LADY AMES *has backed* FORTESCUE *round in an arc towards the bed*. FORTESCUE *looks down unhappily at the crisp inviting sheets*.

LADY AMES. Do you love her?

FORTESCUE. We've loved each other for eleven years.

LADY AMES. You've been away for ten.

FORTESCUE Well, yes... but I wrote...

LADY AMES. You wrote?

FORTESCUE. Letters...

LADY AMES. Does she excite you?

FORTESCUE. And... er... postcards.

LADY AMES. If you're going to marry her... she must excite you deeply, passionately...

FORTESCUE. She's not that sort of girl. She has other qualities...

LADY AMES. Such as...

FORTESCUE. She's a very good organiser.

LADY AMES. That's not enough.

FORTESCUE *(lamely)*. It's a start...

LADY AMES. You want more, don't you, that's why you came here...

FORTESCUE. I want help to start the Mission.

LADY AMES. I'm offering you help.

FORTESCUE *(her face is close against his . . . their bodies touching)*. But I can't give *you* anything . . .

LADY AMES. If you *do*, I can give you everything.

FORTESCUE *(with a final effort of will power)*. In that case, I must regretfully refuse.

He makes for the door, grabbing his briefcase as he does so. Suddenly they both freeze as they hear footsteps approaching up the passage.

FORTESCUE *(in horror)*. Who's that?

LADY AMES. Oh my God! . . . get into bed . . .

FORTESCUE. What about you?

LADY AMES. I'll get in as well.

FORTESCUE. Do you think that's a good idea?

LADY AMES. Quickly . . .

FORTESCUE. Oh dear God . . .

He flies across to the bed and climbs in. LADY AMES *follows.*

LADY AMES. Be asleep . . .

FORTESCUE. But –

LADY AMES. Ssh . . .

She disappears down the bed. FORTESCUE *gives a look of extreme helplessness, then shuts his eyes tight.*

The footsteps come nearer and nearer. The handle turns and the door opens. SLATTERTHWAITE, *the butler, enters, humming to himself. He shuts the door and pauses, sighing with the blessed relief of another hard day over. He takes off his tie and hangs it on the mirror. Then he removes his coat and hangs it up on the back of the door. He loosens his starched white shirt front, and begins to get out of his shirt.*

FORTESCUE, *in bed, opens one eye as much as he dares; what he sees fills him with great apprehension. The eye shuts.* SLATTERTHWAITE *removes his shirt and goes to lay it on a chair when he stops. He looks down at the shoes and clothes already there. He looks around the room, shakes his head in irritation, picks up the shirt, takes the tie and coat, and tiptoes out.*

The door closes.

FORTESCUE *(in a relieved whisper)*. He's gone . . .

Then, in some alarm, as nothing happens . . .

FORTESCUE. Lady Ames, he's *gone*! *(There is a languid movement down the bed.)* Oh, dear!

Meanwhile, in a vast, dismal, sepulchral chamber in another part of the house, on a huge double bed, LORD AMES *lies, propped up against satin pillows. He is reading* Discipline in the Turkish Army 1587–1603: The Savage Years. *There is a light knock and he looks up to see* SLATTERTHWAITE *enter, in stockinged feet, half undressed and clutching his clothes, as he'd left* FORTESCUE's *bedroom.*

SLATTERTHWAITE. Sorry, your Lordship . . . I turned right at the top of the stairs instead of left.

LORD AMES *(laying aside his huge tome and patting the bed next to him irritably)*. All right . . . hurry up!

NARRATOR. So, with an act of typical dedication, Fortescue finally ensured that the Mission to Fallen Women became a reality. From now on he was to dedicate his evangelical energies into a new and unfamiliar world – the violent streets of London's dockland.

London's dockland. A few weeks later.

Outside a corner pub a prostitute grabs her child and takes it home. Another comes out of the pub with two sailors reeling drunkenly on either arm. This trio make their way between run-down dingy houses. The sailors stop at the doors to the Mission to Seamen and try to drag the girl in. She pulls herself away with a laugh.

PROSTITUTE. Oh, no, we've got our very own mission now.

She makes a rude noise and a mock curtsey to a house across the road. It's in a very poor state of repair, needs painting, and one of the windows is broken. A recently painted sign reads: 'The Church of England Mission to Fallen Women.'

Inside it is well swept, but with bare boards, roughly applied distemper on the walls, a fire and about half a dozen camp beds.

FORTESCUE *sits alone at a rickety trestle table, writing a letter. A stone hits the window and an obscenity rings raucously up from the street. He stops and reads what he has written.*

FORTESCUE. Dear Deborah, Thank you for your letter of the 18th. Reference DF 471/106B. Yes, of course you were right to send me back to the Ameses, and I am, as you say, much more financially secure now. I have spent a week cleaning up the house and now I am going out to find our first Fallen Woman ... *(He crosses that out.)* lady tramp. I hope all goes well with the wedding preparations. I remain your dearest fiancé, Charles ...

He signs the letter with a flourish, picks it up, folds it and slips it into an envelope which he licks and seals, then he takes off his apron, rolls down his sleeves, reaches for his coat and hat. He checks his appearance in the mirror, takes a last look around the room, picks up the letter and, glancing once more at the immoral world beckoning outside, makes for the door.

FORTESCUE *comes out of the Mission House. He crosses the road, drops his letter in the post box and sets off in search of sin.*

There is plenty to choose from in this particular stretch of dockland. Various devious characters hang around doorways, and there are a number of sailors wandering hopefully through this twilight world.

His eye is caught by the sight of a large, voluptuous, rather motherly whore coming out of a doorway across the street. FORTESCUE *watches her from the shadows, fascinated.*

LARGE PROSTITUTE (ADA). Come on!

The figure of a very small, limping, old man comes out, reluctantly, after her.

LITTLE OLD MAN *(protesting)*. I've got another twenty minutes ...

ADA *(tolerantly)*. What would you do with another twenty minutes ...?

LITTLE OLD MAN *(eyes lighting up)*. I've just thought of something.

ADA. Go away!

LITTLE OLD MAN. I've always wanted to have a go at it ...

ADA. Well, life's too short, isn't it? ... Now bugger off ...

The LITTLE OLD MAN, *with a contemptuous growl, limps off into the crowd, muttering.* FORTESCUE *licks his lips, swallows hard and makes his way with difficulty across the busy street, reaching* ADA *as she takes up position again in her doorway.*

FORTESCUE. May I speak to you?

A face turns towards him with a frown, then as he emerges from the darkness, it changes to a warmer smile.

ADA. Yeah, all right ... come on ...

She indicates the door.

FORTESCUE *enters and follows her up some stairs ... He flinches, in some disgust, at the noise and the filth of the staircase. Shouts of an argument and a smashing of bottles from inside one of the rooms.*

They enter a small room.

ADA. Sorry about the climb. Hope it's worth it.

ADA *starts to unbutton.*

FORTESCUE *(quickly)*. No ... no ... I really do just want to talk ...

ADA. I'll have to charge you ...

FORTESCUE. Yes, I have some money ...

ADA. Well, we'll have a chat and then if you want something later I'll include it all in the price – it's five shillings for an hour ...

He hands it over.

ADA. Thank you ...

She goes to a little Chinese lacquer box, brought from the Orient by one of her regulars, and puts the money away, tidily.

ADA. It's funny. I like the clergy. I've never once been roughed up or cheated by a man of the cloth. I wasn't much of a churchgoer when I was young but since I've been obliging vicars I've gained a lot of respect for them ... Now then, what's your problem?

ADA *lays her hand gently on his face.*

FORTESCUE. Well, I have no problem ... er ... I'm here as a representative of the Bishop of London and the Church Missionary Society ... (ADA's *smile fades.*) ... and we are opening a Mission house up the road in order that ...

ADA *(wearily, almost bitterly)*. 'Mortal sinners like ourselves can be turned away from the dark paths of wickedness and promiscuity ...' (FORTESCUE *is about to speak.*) Listen, I've been working this patch nineteen years, Reverend. I know all the sins I'm committing which

66

is more than can be said for some of you lot who come round here to try and save us every three weeks ... (FORTESCUE *again makes to speak, but* ADA *is in full flow.*) 'Love one another' – that's what He said, isn't it?

FORTESCUE. Yes ...

ADA. So that's what I do. Oh, you get the odd one with a funny idea or two, but most of my boys just want company, a bit of warmth, a bit of cheering up. I'm like a mother to 'em – only they can't fuck their mothers so they come here, excuse my language but that's how they talk around here, take it or leave it.

She pulls open the door, FORTESCUE *rises.*

FORTESCUE. I don't disapprove of you.

ADA *(with a mirthless laugh)*. Of course not. You just disapprove of what we do, what we – *(She mimics.)* – 'indulge in'. That's the trouble with your lot . . . You 'ate sex. You never 'ave it, so you 'ate it.

FORTESCUE. That's not true.

ADA. 'Course it is. As soon as you come in you say 'I'm not here for sexual reasons.' As if there's something wrong with anyone who *is* . . .

FORTESCUE. Well, *(Fingering his hat.)* I don't really think that way . . .

ADA *(slowly closing the door)*. All right! If I was to say to you . . . You're a nice-looking feller . . . How about a quick one? . . . What would you say?

FORTESCUE. Well . . . I'd think about it.

ADA *stops. This isn't the answer she'd expected. She stands and regards* FORTESCUE, *but in a different light this time.* FORTESCUE *returns her look evenly. The two stand without speaking for a while.*

ADA *(slowly and deliberately with the hint of a triumphal smile)*. All right, then . . . You're a nice-looking feller, how about a quick one?

FORTESCUE*'s expression doesn't change for a moment. Then a couple of rapid blinks indicate that he is considering his options and realises he only has one. He says nothing for rather a long time whilst his brain wrestles to reconcile theological, moral and ethical considerations with his ever-present and all-consuming curiosity.*

After what seems an eternity and without another word exchanged, FORTESCUE *carefully lowers his hat and lays it on the table.*

The Church of England Mission to Fallen Women. Some days later.

The place is now a hive of activity. There are ex-scrubbers everywhere scrubbing floors, cleaning, polishing, tidying . . . In the middle of all this is FORTESCUE, *dog-collared, eyes shining with a renewed sense of purpose, directing them to do this and that. Moving furniture. Helping to bring more beds in from outside. Business is booming. Clearly the girls admire him almost inordinately.*

NARRATOR. Word of Fortescue's unique blend of moral leadership and personal availability spread like wildfire through the back streets of East London. Within three weeks of its opening the Mission house was filled to capacity. But as the day of his wedding approached, Fortescue was finding the work increasingly demanding.

Beneath a faded picture of Edward the Seventh, and an equally dusty crucifix, FORTESCUE, *eyes dark-rimmed from exhaustion, lies asleep in his ascetic little room. There is a very light knock followed by silence. Followed by a bolder knock.* FORTESCUE *wakes. He strains to look at the clock on the chair beside his bed. Another knock.*

FORTESCUE. Come in . . .

A young girl enters. It's very dark and we can only make out a shape at the door.

FORTESCUE. Hello . . . who's that?

GIRL. Emmeline, sir.

FORTESCUE. Ah yes.

EMMELINE. You know you said about coming to see you with problems?

FORTESCUE. Well, I meant in the morning, really.

EMMELINE. Well, I can't sleep because of this problem.

FORTESCUE. What is it?

EMMELINE. I keep thinking about you.

FORTESCUE *(rubbing his eyes)*. About me ... *(He laughs.)* ... Well, I shouldn't waste your time doing that...

EMMELINE. You're not like anyone I've ever met. *(There is a slight pause.)* It's just that most of the people I've been to bed with didn't care who I was ... you know ...

FORTESCUE. Ah yes ... I *do* know, and I only wish that more girls like you would realise this, and not try and glamorise what they do...

EMMELINE. Yes ... I agree with you, sir ... really. I mean, I'd just love to go to bed with someone who was kind and considerate and gentle, just once, you know ...

FORTESCUE. Well, I'm glad you feel like that, because this is what our Mission is all about...

EMMELINE *(coming close to him.)* Oh, wonderful . . .

She begins to pull off the rough smock she's wearing as a nightdress.

FORTESCUE *(grabbing the sheets)*. What are you doing?

EMMELINE *(sliding into bed)*. There's so many preachers around telling you what to do . . . give up this, give up that . . . none of 'em ever show you a better way, you know . . . Mm it's warm . . .

She snuggles down in the bed and looks up at FORTESCUE *who sits bolt upright clutching the sheet. He looks down at her.*

FORTESCUE. Emmeline . . . let me just explain what I mean. You mustn't confuse the sexual act with moral and spiritual values . . .

EMMELINE. What does that mean?

FORTESCUE *(wearily)*. It means that physical sex is not necessarily that important.

EMMELINE. That's just what I always said. Do it and enjoy it. It's not the end of the world . . .

FORTESCUE. No . . . I don't think you've quite grasped what I mean. St Paul says something rather interesting here . . .

A voice from the darkness.

VOICE. Emmeline, you cow!

FORTESCUE. Who's that?

VOICE. Agnes, sir . . .

ANOTHER VOICE. And Louise . . .

Two other girls, with candles, approach from the door.

FORTESCUE *(pulling the sheet up even more)*. Ah . . . Agnes . . . Louise . . . come in . . . *(With as much dignity as he can muster.)* I was just telling Emmeline how relatively unimportant sex is . . .

AGNES and LOUISE. Ooh . . . good . . .

There is a rustling of falling nightgowns and some girlish cries as they clamber into his bed.

At *that same moment, in the rectory at Little Fidding,* DEBORAH *sits at a table which is full of piles of invitations, seating plans, etc. She is, of course, sorting things into boxes. She picks a letter out of an envelope.*

DEBORAH *(to herself)*. Campions . . . two . . . fourth row . . . bridegroom's side . . . 24.6.06 . . .

She makes notes on a seating plan, ticks off the name on two lists, drops the letter into a box and briskly goes on to the next.

DEBORAH. Mr and Mrs Napier and Amanda . . . row seven . . . bride's side . . . B14 . . . 23.6.06.

FITZBANKS. Absolutely still now, petal . . .

She looks up. We see that FITZBANKS *has a complicated camera with a flash attachment set up in the middle of the room.* PARSWELL *stands between* DEBORAH *and the camera, holding up a gilt frame.*

DEBORAH. Oh, Daddy, d'you have to?

FITZBANKS *(pottering with the camera)*. It'll be jolly interesting in years to come for people to see how we lived.

DEBORAH. *Not* when I'm doing my seating plan.

FITZBANKS. Young girl preparing for her wedding!

There is a flash.

The Mission *in the morning. Up the dingy East End street, with a clattering and a clamour comes a most elegant and expensive coach and pair, with wide-eyed street kids following along in its wake. They've seen nothing like this before.*

In it sits LADY AMES, *looking around with ill-concealed distaste at the dirt and squalor around her. Her coach pulls up in front of the Mission. The usual gaggle of kids and onlookers scramble around it. The driver runs round and opens the door.* LADY AMES *alights.*

She walks up the steps, quickly arranging her hat and hair as she does so. She looks absolutely stunning and completely out of place.

There being no bell, LADY AMES *pushes the door open.*

LADY AMES *(calling)*. Charles?

A couple of girls are cleaning out the fireplace. One turns, then the other. They stare open-mouthed at her.

LADY AMES. Is the Reverend Fortescue here?

The girls nod, still tongue-tied by the sight of such wealth and beauty.

LADY AMES. Well, I'd like to see him, please.

VIOLET. Er ... he's upstairs asleep ma'am ...

LADY AMES. It's ten o'clock!

VIOLET. Yes, ... er, I'll go and see ...

LADY AMES. I think he should be awake by now, don't you?

She sets off up the stairs, briskly.

VIOLET *(getting up)*. Er ...

But it's too late. We see LADY AMES *playfully knock on a door marked 'Reverend Fortescue'.*

There is no sound from within.

She knocks again a little louder.

This time FORTESCUE's *voice answers, but it's weak and tired.*

FORTESCUE. Look ... I can't deal with any more problems tonight girls ... Please. Just let me sleep for an hour ...

LADY AMES *opens the door a crack and peeps in.*

LADY AMES. Charles?

The word dies on her lips as she beholds the scene.

Three naked girls lie stretched out on FORTESCUE's *bed, beautifully asleep. On the floor, beside the bed, with a rough blanket over him, is the dishevelled figure of* FORTESCUE *in a crumpled nightshirt.*

FORTESCUE *opens an eye blearily and unwillingly. Then as he registers who it is, sits bolt upright, as if the KGB had just applied 3000 volts to the soles of his feet.*

FORTESCUE. Isabel! Hello...

    LADY AMES *just stares at the contents of the bed, then at* FORTESCUE. *Then she shuts the door, and stands outside.*

FORTESCUE. Isabel!

    From inside the room come the sounds of thumps, bangs and muffled imprecations of someone trying to dress in a state of hysterical panic. Eventually the door opens and FORTESCUE *rushes out trying to fasten his dog collar on with difficulty.*

FORTESCUE. Isabel ... how nice to see you ... oh *how* nice ... Er ... it's all going terribly well ... as you can see, the overcrowding's a major problem ... I even had to give up my bed ... Isabel!

    She turns on her heel and walks downstairs. He hurries after her. She turns at the bottom of the stairs.

LADY AMES. I'm sorry to have disturbed you! I didn't know you were so involved in your work.

FORTESCUE. Isabel! Look ... You can't just go ... now you've come all this way.

LADY AMES. I'm in the way ... I can tell when I'm in the way ...

FORTESCUE *(to the open-mouthed girls cleaning the grate)*. Er ... Vicky ...

VIOLET. Violet, sir ...

FORTESCUE. Violet ... Could you and Ruby ...

SECOND GIRL. Rosy ...

FORTESCUE. – Rosy, go and clean upstairs please ... and will you get ... er ... er ... *(He tries to remember the names and can't.)* ... those three girls in my bed to help you ...

    This doesn't improve matters with LADY AMES. FORTESCUE *makes after her desperately.*

FORTESCUE (*with forced brightness*). Well, what do you think of it?

LADY AMES (*looking around*). It's . . . er . . . very nice for you.

FORTESCUE. Isabel, what's the matter?

LADY AMES. The matter?

FORTESCUE. Well, you sound rather . . . er . . . well, less than happy about something. Is it the mess?

LADY AMES. Listen . . . since that night at Moretonhampstead, I haven't seen or heard of you. You haven't visited me, and the one time I decide to visit *you*, I find everyone sleeping in one bed – yours!

FORTESCUE. I can explain that *quite* easily . . .

LADY AMES. Oh, I'm sure you can . . . you're a missionary. That's what you're trained for, isn't it? To 'explain' things to people . . .

FORTESCUE. Isabel . . . these girls have had no love or affection in their lives . . . I have to listen to them, I have to be prepared to spend time with them . . .

LADY AMES. It must be awful for you.

FORTESCUE. Isabel . . . what is wrong with you?

LADY AMES. Do you *ever* think of me . . .?

FORTESCUE. Of course I think of you. I thought of you on Tuesday. I was going to put your name on the sign. The Lady Ames Mission for . . .

LADY AMES (*closes her eyes in exasperation*). Oh!

    FORTESCUE *looks hurt.*

FORTESCUE. What do you want?

LADY AMES. I thought our lives were going to change after that night.

FORTESCUE. Well mine *has* changed . . . I mean that night made a great difference to me Isabel . . .

LADY AMES (*reaching in her bag*). So I see.

    She holds up what is unmistakably a wedding invitation.

FORTESCUE (*brightly*). Oh yes . . . the invitation, that's Deborah . . . She's awfully keen on you.

LADY AMES (*with a mixture of anger and tears*). You can't *do* this to me Charles! You can't unlock the door and then run away . . .

FORTESCUE (*genuinely confused*). Isabel?

LADY AMES. I give you fair warning that if *you're* not going to help me change my life, I shall change it myself. (*She turns on her heel and makes for the door.*) I shall start with the bank account. If you're doing so well you won't need *my* money any longer.

FORTESCUE. Isabel . . . listen . . .

    MAUDE *runs up.*

MAUDE. Reverend . . .?

LADY AMES. . . . and the answer is 'No thank you'.

    She pushes the wedding invitation back into his hands.

FORTESCUE. Isabel!

MAUDE. Reverend!

FORTESCUE *(with irritation)*. What is it?

    LADY AMES *goes out, slamming the door.*

MAUDE *(pulling down her dress to reveal scratched shoulder)*. It's bleeding, look. That's bloody Lizzy Carpenter's boot, that is!

LIZZY *(rushing up to* FORTESCUE*)*. She took my bed . . . put her things all over it.

MAUDE. It was my bloody bed, Reverend said *I* could have the one by the window.

    LIZZY *goes for* MAUDE. FORTESCUE *struggles to keep them apart. As he does so, he watches helplessly as* LADY AMES's *vehicle disappears.*

FORTESCUE *(desperately, from the window)*. Isabel! . . . Isabel . . . please come back!

NARRATOR. The withdrawal of Lady Ames' funds was a serious blow for the Mission to Fallen Women. But such was their regard for Fortescue that the inmates voluntarily decided to go back on to the streets to raise money.

From the Mission door a number of girls appear; they are dressed up for trade and are being well drilled by their leader, LIZZIE.

LIZZIE. Grace . . . you take the High Street first shift. Maude, High Street second shift. Emmy . . . graveyard first shift, Louise, graveyard second shift . . .

And so on.

NARRATOR. Sure enough, as the nights went by, the Mission survived but only to face another, far more serious threat . . .

A few days later on the roof of the Mission FORTESCUE *and the girls are pegging freshly-washed underwear on to parallel clothes-lines. A scene of bustle and activity, with some girls carrying out baskets and others holding up the fresh laundry for others to peg. Everyone seems rushed off their feet, but enjoying themselves.*

FORTESCUE. Julie . . . take the other end and . . . *(He suddenly stops and looks up)* . . . Bishop!

There, indeed, between a girdle and a large pair of knickers stands the BISHOP OF LONDON.

BISHOP *(with mock jollity)*. Don't let me hold up the . . . er . . . the good work . . .

FORTESCUE *(laughs)*. Oh, that's all right, there's plenty of willing hands . . . Here Jane . . .

He hands over the washing.

JUNE. June.

BISHOP. How are you?

FORTESCUE *(with pride)*. Twenty-eight girls last night sir . . .

BISHOP *(uncertainly)*. Good . . . good . . .

FORTESCUE. And I want to get as much done as I can before the wedding.

BISHOP. Tomorrow, isn't it?

FORTESCUE. That's right . . . it's sort of crept up on me.

The BISHOP's *face clouds.*

BISHOP *(aside to* FORTESCUE*)*. Fortescue, can we talk somewhere, old chap . . . somewhere away from the crowd . . . D'you have a room?

FORTESCUE. Yes, but the girls are in there . . . *(Noting the* BISHOP's *raised eyebrows)* . . . painting it while I'm away. Out here's as quiet as anywhere.

BISHOP. Well . . .

He looks around, a little discomfited at having to talk amongst steaming washing.

FORTESCUE. Girls! Give us a couple of minutes . . .

The girls go, one or two giving the BISHOP *rich smiles as they pass, which embarrasses him further. One of the girls is still working away at a mangle.*

FORTESCUE. Agnes! *(She looks up.)* Give us two minutes, please.

He turns to the BISHOP.

FORTESCUE. Now what can I do for you, my Lord?

AGNES *stands in front of them, a little puzzled, but provocatively gazing up at the* BISHOP.

FORTESCUE *(hastily)*. No . . . no . . . Agnes. Two minutes to *talk*, please.

AGNES *gradually catches on that her services are not required, looks a trifle disappointed, and goes away.* FORTESCUE *indicates to the* BISHOP *and they walk away from the stairs, occasionally losing each other between the underwear.*

BISHOP. I . . . er . . . I just dropped in actually on my way back from a Missionary Council meeting.

FORTESCUE *(modestly)*. I should imagine they must be rather pleased . . .

BISHOP. Well, they're a funny lot ... you know how ... competitive the churches are these days ...

FORTESCUE. Hockey, my lord ...?

BISHOP. No ... no ... no ... religion.

FORTESCUE. Oh yes ...

BISHOP. Well to be quite blunt ... we've had complaints of unfair competition from other religions er ... in the area ... The Catholics, Methodists, Unitarians, Anabaptists – they've all had to close Missions – can't get the girls.

FORTESCUE. Well, that's a feather in our cap ... isn't it?

BISHOP. It's the grounds of the complaints, I'm afraid.

FORTESCUE. What grounds?

The BISHOP *pauses and looks at* FORTESCUE *carefully for a moment.*

BISHOP *(hesitantly).* I think you should pad up, Fortescue, I'm going to bowl you some rather fast ... balls ...

He reaches into his briefcase. At that moment two girls with washing come chasing out into the yard, clearly unaware that anyone else is there. They pull up with a cry of fright at the sight of the two clerics in the corner of the yard.

FORTESCUE *(nodding to the back door).* Thank you, girls ...

The girls nod and run back inside. We hear a shriek of suppressed laughter as the roof door opens and shuts. The BISHOP *looks even more uncomfortable. He opens a small black notebook he's taken from his briefcase and clears his throat.*

BISHOP *(reading).* Father D'Arcy of the Society of Jesus claims he knows for certain that you have had – *(The* BISHOP *pauses, and breathes in heavily here.)* – sexual dealings with a Miss Ada Shields a well-known and apparently unrepentant lady of the streets, lodging at 41G Willis Buildings ... Mr Pinney of the First Risen Church of God says that girls who used to come to him, now go to you, because you offer them, er, sexual favours ... Mr Hardy of the Hackney Street Methodist Community Hall says he has seen you through the window 'helping girls'.

FORTESCUE. My lord. Let me explain ...

BISHOP. No need to, old boy ... no need to. *I* know it's not true, but once tongues start wagging ...

FORTESCUE *looks worried. The* BISHOP *starts to walk back through the washing.*

BISHOP. Look, I'm your greatest supporter. You've played a cracking innings here, but I think the time has come, especially on the eve of your marriage, to think of moving on.

FORTESCUE *(incredulously)*. Moving on?

BISHOP. We've found an excellent successor . . . a lady of great character. Thoroughly trained in the prison service.

FORTESCUE. I can't leave the girls . . .

BISHOP. I'm afraid it's either that or the Missionary Council close the place down and consider disciplinary action of some sort . . . and that's not worth it with a career like yours, now is it, old chap? I'll lay you an odds on bet you could be a bishop yourself in five years.

FORTESCUE. Me, a bishop . . .?

BISHOP. Oh yes . . . if you play your cards right . . . *(Leaning towards him confidentially.)* I have it on very high authority . . . One of the better dioceses – nothing too industrial.

FORTESCUE *(thoughtfully, but with a hint of bitterness)*. Well . . . I suppose that would be much more up Deborah's street. She's always been rather keen on the ecclesiastical life – the big old house swarming with children.

BISHOP. Absolutely, and who wouldn't be?

They've reached the back door. The BISHOP *clearly regards the whole thing as solved. He pats* FORTESCUE *on the shoulder encouragingly, and opens the roof door.*

BISHOP. Well . . . I must be on my way . . . got an exorcism in Chiswick.

As they walk down the stairs towards the front door, he turns to FORTESCUE.

BISHOP. Talking of big old houses, I was sorry to hear about our friend Lady Ames.

FORTESCUE. Oh, well, we've coped perfectly well without her money sir . . . almost better –

BISHOP. No, I meant the nasty business down at Moretonhampstead yesterday.

FORTESCUE. What business?

BISHOP. Oh, rather unpleasant. Someone poisoned the food. One of the gardeners died outright . . .

FORTESCUE. Oh, how dreadful . . .

BISHOP. Well, it could have been worse. The food was apparently intended for Lord Ames himself, but the butler took the wrong turning . . .

FORTESCUE stops. His face creases into a sudden expression of deep alarm.

They've reached the front door. The BISHOP *pulls it open.*

BISHOP. Well . . . pip, pip . . . See you at the wedding . . . Oh, and cheer up. I think you've made the right decision.

He smiles at FORTESCUE *paternally, pats his shoulder again and leaves, pushing the kids aside with un-Christian force.* FORTESCUE *doesn't say goodbye. He stands on the doorstep, deeply worried by the news of the Ames' poisoning. . . . As the* BISHOP's *carriage disappears up the street* FORTESCUE's *look of confused fear and alarm is replaced by one of mounting determination.* LADY AMES' *words come back to his mind:* 'I give you fair warning . . . if you're not going to help me change my life I shall change it myself.'

Moretonhampstead Hall stands serenely in the mellow evening light when the silence of twilight is broken by the sound of a coach and pair, driven hard, sweeping up the long driveway. Inside the coach FORTESCUE *can hardly wait for it to come to a halt, before jumping down and hurrying up the steps to the door. He raps hard on the knocker;* SLATTERTHWAITE *appears after a pause.*

SLATTERTHWAITE. Ah, morning sir. The dog . . .

FORTESCUE. What?

SLATTERTHWAITE. The dog awaits . . .

SLATTERTHWAITE *steps back into the hall and reappears with a well manicured little King Charles spaniel sitting in a basket.*

SLATTERTHWAITE. Mr Carlton the under-footman will collect on Tuesday . . .

FORTESCUE. Don't you remember me?

SLATTERTHWAITE. Yes of course sir . . . you are Mr Emanuel the dog-clipper from Faversham.

FORTESCUE. No, my name is Fortescue. The missionary. I stayed here once.

SLATTERTHWAITE *(with a great effort of recall)*. Medium height, dark hair with a moustache and a dog-collar?

FORTESCUE. That's me, yes. I must see Lady Ames please . . .

SLATTERTHWAITE. I'm afraid you can't sir . . .

FORTESCUE. It *is* very urgent.

SLATTERTHWAITE. I'm afraid she isn't here sir. After the unfortunate attempt on her husband's life she insisted on taking him away with her. To recover from the shock.

FORTESCUE *(with urgency)*. She's taken him away?

SLATTERTHWAITE. To shoot . . .

FORTESCUE. What?

SLATTERTHWAITE. At Carnoustie House . . . in Scotland, sir . . . one of their Scottish homes . . .

FORTESCUE. Where is it?

SLATTERTHWAITE. Oh, you can't miss it, sir. Either left or right out of the station.

FORTESCUE. Thank you. Thank you very much.

SLATTERTHWAITE. Not at all sir . . .

   FORTESCUE *turns to go.*

SLATTERTHWAITE. And you're sure you're not Mr Emanuel from Faversham?

FORTESCUE *(with some irritation).* No . . . no. My name is *Fortescue.*

SLATTERTHWAITE. Ah! *You're* Fortescue. *(He steps back indoors, lays the dog down and picks up a note.)* In that case I must point out that I am under strict instructions from her ladyship, not to . . . tell you . . . er . . . that . . . *(He peers at the paper uncomprehendingly.)*

FORTESCUE *(helpfully).* That she is at Carnoustie House, near Pitlochry.

SLATTERTHWAITE *(with relief).* Ah yes, that's right, sir.

FORTESCUE. Thank you.

SLATTERTHWAITE. Not at all, sir.

   He bows with dignity and closes the front door. Unfortunately he hasn't gone in yet. He is left ringing the doorbell, rather pathetically. Somewhere in the house an aristocratic dog barks.

NARRATOR. And so it was, on the very morning of his wedding that Charles Fortescue found himself on a life or death mission five hundred miles away in the Highlands of Scotland.

Next morning. The REVEREND FORTESCUE, *a lone figure, strains at the oars of a small rowing boat. He pulls with great urgency then turns to look towards a rambling, turreted, unmistakably Scottish seat, Carnoustie House. At the front of the house four gleaming new Lanchester cars are drawn up in the drive, together with a selection of other more traditional conveyances. A distant cock crows.*

F̲irst light in the village of Little Fidding. Everywhere is silent and asleep. A flock of geese is suddenly disturbed by something in a farmyard. They yell and screech for a moment. PARSWELL, *goose in hand, lumbers off towards the kitchen of the Rectory.*

At an upstairs window, the curtains are drawn back revealing DEBORAH. *She cranes her neck excitedly to see the state of the day's weather. She gives a deep breath and a smile of approval, for it is indeed going to be a lovely day for a wedding . . .*

B̲ack at Carnoustie House a line of servants, bearing crates of champagne, quails egg sandwiches, and bowls and plates groaning with stuffed pheasant, boar's head, wren pâté and all manner of delicacies, are being marshalled by a tough humourless little Scottish major-domo, CORBETT. *He directs them to take their wares to the various conveyances.*

CORBETT. Champagne . . . Car Two! Cold Roast Beef . . . Car Four! Pheasant . . . Car Four! Quails in Aspic Car . . . Four! Caviar . . . *(He looks around.) Caviar! . . . Who* is transporting the caviar!

The wretched servants — mainly rather fresh-faced young boys, indicate a particularly thin and weedy colleague. CORBETT *goes up to him, glaring and lifts the linen napkin off the dish he's holding.*

CORBETT. This is not caviar . . . d'you understand?

The thin and weedy BOY *nods his head fearfully.*

CORBETT. You know what caviar looks like?

The thin and weedy BOY *nods.*

CORBETT *takes the plate from him.*

CORBETT. Right . . . well return to the kitchen and if you come out here again without caviar I shall personally kick your stupid little head right across the fucking loch! Ah . . . good morning, your ladyship . . .

The thin and weedy BOY *retreats terrified just as the first members of a very upper-class hunting party emerge into the crisp early morning air.*

LADY QUIMBY. Morning Corbett.

LORD QUIMBY *(elderly and distinguished)*. Morning Corbett.

CORBETT *(unctuously)*. A marvellous day for the sport, m'lud . . .

LORD QUIMBY. Yes thank you . . . indeed.

CORBETT *smiles, gives a half bow and walks away to the cars.*

LADY QUIMBY. Henry's frightfully lucky to have a chap like Corbett . . .

LORD QUIMBY. Oh yes . . . salt of the earth . . .

Soon the remaining members of the hunting party start to emerge. Drifting on the still air there is a dawn chorus of 'Good morning', 'Morning', 'Mor-ning' etc. They are plus-foured and the women and the men tend to stand in separate groups. They represent a classic selection of the chinly deprived classes.

FORTESCUE *meanwhile is rowing ever closer across the loch.*

The hunting party take in the freshness of the Scottish morning and the splendours of the house and its setting.

FIRST YOUNG MAN *(who's obviously a first time guest)*. I say . . . it is a marvellous place, isn't it . . .?

SECOND YOUNG MAN. Absolutely *splendid* . . .

FIRST YOUNG MAN. *Absolutely* splendid.

(After a pause to appreciate the beauties of the Scottish countryside.)

FIRST YOUNG MAN. Did you manage to find a lavatory?

SECOND YOUNG MAN. No . . .

FIRST YOUNG MAN *(a little regretfully)*. No . . . nor me . . .

A slightly older pair, the DUKE OF PORTLAND *and the* EARL OF LEICESTER *emerge from the front door, talking.*

LEICESTER. Pity old Raggy Masterson couldn't make it up here.

PORTLAND. Yes, damn shame. Still, you only give leopards one chance.

LEICESTER. Damn lucky he was wearing his medals.

PORTLAND. Well, he always does . . . Raggy wears his Empire Cross in bed, so Celia tells me . . .

LEICESTER. What's that enormous medal one gets for being frightfully well connected?

PORTLAND. K. C. V. G.

LEICESTER. That's it. Well, Raggy's K.C.V.G. got stuck in the creature's gizzard. Leopard threw up, and a great deal of Raggy was saved . . .

There is a commotion at the door. They turn. LORD AMES *and* LADY AMES *appear.* LADY AMES *looks resplendently overdressed as usual. Much hat doffing.*

At the other side of the house FORTESCUE *has guided his boat ashore. He leaps out and makes for the house.*

87

A rich Asian potentate – turbanned, and plus-foured – the MAHARAJAH OF JUDAPUR *has joined* LORD *and* LADY AMES. *He has his gun, but appears to be nearly blind and is being led by a native boy.*

MAHARAJAH. Morning!

Much doffing of hats.

EVERYONE. Morning, your Highness . . . Morning Maharajah.

LORD AMES *(taking the* MAHARAJAH's *arm).* This way old chap . . .

He helps guide the shuffling, beaming, myopic, Indian towards the cars.

MAHARAJAH. How big are the grouse?

LORD AMES. The grouse? . . . oh they're quite big . . .

MAHARAJAH. Good . . . good . . . *(He beams politely).* I can only kill the larger birds now.

FAWNING YOUNG MAN *(catching up with Ames).* I love the cars, sir . . .

LORD AMES *(abstractedly).* Yes . . . yes . . . I thought I ought to get a few . . . Come on everyone . . . don't want the champagne to get warm . . .

Horsey laughter and general movement towards the cars.

FORTESCUE *rounds the corner of the house just in time to see* LADY AMES, *who is waiting on the steps and doesn't seem to be joining the main group.*

LADY AMES. I'll join you all later. Mr Corbett and I have some business things to sort out . . . Quite tedious . . . *(A few sycophantic groans from some of the men.)* Oh, don't sound so frightfully disappointed . . . I know what you men *really* think of women in the field . . . They only get in the way . . .

Polite laughter and fawning protestations.

The party move to the cars and coaches. Servants bustling around them all the time, opening car doors. Holding guns while the nobility clamber in.

PORTLAND *(to* LEICESTER, *nodding in* LADY AMES' *direction).* Who's she *with* at the moment?

LEICESTER. No idea, been keeping herself to herself recently, rather withdrawn from society . . . you know . . .

PORTLAND. I expected to see Cholmondeley creeping around here I must say.

LEICESTER. Oh no, he only shoots with the Royals, nowadays . . .

PORTLAND. Jocelyn Cholmondeley! How low can they stoop . . .?

He puts his arms out to be helped up into his vehicle.

LEICESTER. He got shot in the hip by the King last week. Couldn't say anything of course. Had to crawl around all day pretending nothing had happened . . . screamed for four hours in the evening though . . .

LEICESTER *is hoisted up into one of the Lanchesters.* CORBETT *barks an order. The four uniformed chauffeurs bend to the starting handles in unison. Another order is barked. They all turn in unison and the cars bark to life in unison. Cheers from the men. Squeals of delight from the women. They move off.*

Meanwhile, back at Little Fidding, the REVEREND FITZBANKS *emerges from his house on this lovely morning and ambles across the lawn to the church. He stops, potters, picks up something from the lawn, looks at it with interest and pockets it, and continues through the wicket gate and into the churchyard. We follow him to the door of the church, passing on the way a gardener clipping away at the verges with whom* FITZBANKS *passes the time of day. As he reaches the door of the old church,* FITZBANKS *looks heavenwards and sniffs the air. Then he goes into the church, smiling to himself.*

In Scotland the REVEREND FORTESCUE *chooses his moment then runs at a crouch towards the back of the house.*

He prises up a nearby window and pulls himself up and into the house.

LADY AMES *meanwhile comes back from the front door with* CORBETT. *She looks businesslike and her eyes have a sort of flat, set determination . . .*

LADY AMES. You've taken care of everything, Corbett?

CORBETT. Yes indeed, Madam.

LADY AMES. Nothing can go wrong?

CORBETT. You have my word on it.

LADY AMES. Good . . . good . . .

LADY AMES *busies herself briskly in the hall – checking a map, looking at her watch and checking it against the hall clock.* CORBETT *stands rather close to her.*

CORBETT. I love Jeannie and the wee ones but, you know, there's never been an hour of a day go by without me thinking of you.

LADY AMES *(briskly, abstractedly).* Well that's nice . . .

She crosses to a low chest of drawers and takes out a small flask.

CORBETT. I knew you'd want me for something special . . . I knew the call would come. I've been holding myself . . . in readiness.

LADY AMES *slips the flask into her pocket and crosses past* CORBETT *to a rack of shooting sticks.*

LADY AMES. I shall make it worth your while, Corbett . . .

CORBETT. Och . . . to be rid of that man will be enough for me. To know that our forbidden love can blossom like the wild jasmine on the slopes of Ben Shiel . . .

LADY AMES *(passing him yet again).* No, I meant money, Corbett . . .

She goes into the gun room off the hall. CORBETT *shadows her like a dog.*

CORBETT. Money! What need I of money when I have *you* . . .

At this he leers close to her, and LADY AMES *neatly avoids him.*

LADY AMES (*selecting a gun*). Yes . . . I shall take this one.

CORBETT (*significantly*). And you have *me* . . . I've seen you admiring my body . . . I've seen you glancing at it on hot summer evenings . . .

LADY AMES (*equivocally*). Ah . . .

CORBETT. Oh, I don't mind! I like you to look at it. I've kept it for you. I don't drink, I don't smoke, I eat raw meats and I undergo dreadful physical hardship every winter in order to bring it to a peak of perfection. As finely tempered as coiled steel. D'you want to see it?

LADY AMES (*neatly avoiding him at the door of the gunroom*). Not now, Corbett. We must be up there as soon as they've finished the first champagne break, which, if I know Henry, will be about ten minutes time. Fetch the coaches would you?

CORBETT. Oh, I like it when you give me orders.

LADY AMES (*sharply*). Now!

CORBETT (*with a sigh*). Mm . . .

> *Almost unable to take his eyes from her he turns and disappears towards the back door of the house.* LADY AMES *takes a last look around the hall and we can see she is in quite a high state of tension. She turns and walks upstairs.*
>
> *When she's gone,* FORTESCUE *emerges, checks that the coast is clear and hurries up the stairs after her. He crosses the landing, whose walls are filled with yet more portraits of the great man. He moves cautiously across to the door she's entered. It's a bedroom. He watches as she puts on a short hunting coat and hat, and checks her appearance in the wall mirror. She pauses for a moment in front of the mirror, then reaches in her pocket for the silver flask and, unscrewing the top, raises it to her lips.* FORTESCUE *enters.*

FORTESCUE. Don't do it Isabel.

> LADY AMES *practically chokes, and whips the flask down guiltily as she turns.*

LADY AMES (*in disbelief*). Charles . . .? What are you *doing* here . . .?

FORTESCUE. I've come to stop you.

> LADY AMES *stares at him. She seems unable to say anything. For a moment a hint of hope lights up her face, then as quickly as it came, it vanishes, to be replaced by a sudden unreasoning anger.*

LADY AMES (*turning abruptly away from him*). How dare you! How dare you interfere with my plans . . .

FORTESCUE. You mustn't kill him.

LADY AMES. Why not?

> FORTESCUE *shakes his head wearily.*

LADY AMES. What business is it of yours? Interfering priest . . .

> *She takes a drink from her flask.*

FORTESCUE. You could hang for it . . .

LADY AMES. No one's going to hang! It'll be a simple shooting accident . . .

FORTESCUE. Look, Isabel . . . this is England in nineteen hundred and six . . . we don't go round killing people just because we don't get on with them.

LADY AMES. No, we just endure, don't we . . .? Stiff upper lip, that's the British way . . . I'm sure Africa wasn't like that . . . mm?

FORTESCUE (*a little unconvincingly*). Africa's primitive.

LADY AMES *(heavily)*. Oh yes . . . God save us from being primitive.

FORTESCUE. There's not so much wrong with the British way of life, Isabel. For your class especially.

LADY AMES. My class! This is not my class, Charles . . .

FORTESCUE. You know what I mean . . .

LADY AMES. You don't know what *I* mean.

> *She stops for a moment.* FORTESCUE *looks up. She turns on him provocatively. She goes into a strong and convincing East End accent. It is hard and rather shocking.*

LADY AMES. You alone, sir . . . want some company, clean and cheap . . . Mm . . .? *(She turns back to the mirror.)* I've disguised it well, haven't I . . . I had to . . . the honest tart never gets anywhere . . . No . . . they're not my class. Thank God.

> *A voice from downstairs.*

CORBETT. Your ladyship ... the carriages are here ...

LADY AMES. You go on, Corbett ...

CORBETT. Of course ...

There is the sound of cheerful Scottish whistling from the hallway downstairs, then the slam of the door and silence.

FORTESCUE. Isabel, I ...

LADY AMES. Don't, please. I don't want to be understood. Not now. *(Fiercely she drains the flask.)*

FORTESCUE. What do you think you're going to do? What are you going to gain from it?

She just stares back at him with a bitter smile. Then she moves smartly for the door and although FORTESCUE *recovers quickly and goes after her, she has slammed it.* FORTESCUE *races to the door before she can lock it, and pulls it open.*

He sees LADY AMES *on the landing. As she sees him pursuing she turns away from the top of the stairs and makes for another smaller staircase, leading upwards.* FORTESCUE *races after her. He finds himself chasing the sound of her footsteps up a circular staircase in one of the turrets. He redoubles his efforts then stops. The footsteps ahead of him have stopped. He proceeds more cautiously. The stairs lead up to a small turret room. The door is open.* FORTESCUE *approaches warily.*

He enters the room and looks around. At that moment the door slams and a key turns. He spins round and hurtles to the door. But it's securely locked. All he can hear are footsteps receding down the stairs.

FORTESCUE. Isabel! ... *Isabel!*

As his panic increases there is an air of idyllic calm back at Little Fidding. Wedding guests are beginning to fill the church. Gentle organ music welcomes them. Sun shines through the stained glass on to the flowers. It is a most tranquil little scene. No sign of Charles Bronson anywhere.

Back at Carnoustie House a panting horse pulling one of the empty carriages comes galloping back towards the house, sweeping in a perilous tight curve and swinging to a halt in the back yard. A servant comes out of the back door.

DRIVER OF WAGON *(jumping down, breathlessly)*. More champagne ...

SERVANT. Jesus Christ!

He shakes his head and the two of them disappear into the house.

High on the highest turret of the house the SERVANT OF THE LORD *is standing perilously on a stone water-spout. He edges his way with great difficulty round the tower, occasionally forgetting that the one thing to avoid in such a situation is to look down. Sheer terror grips him.*

Meanwhile, the carriage with LADY AMES *in is bounding over a moorland track.*

LADY AMES *looks out of the window. She sees an expanse of grouse moor stretching below her, set up for a shoot. A dozen butts have been built, and to one side beaters are sitting eating sandwiches, whilst in the middle of it all, a table is set out at which the hunting party are seated. Footmen, in full uniform, attend them, pouring champagne. The rich, braying sound of upper-class laughter drifts across the moor.* LADY AMES *looks anxiously off to one side.*

On another part of the moor CORBETT *heads his horse off the road and across bumpy tussocky grass towards a rise, on the other side of which the shoot is taking place.*

He slows, dismounts, tethers the horse to a piece of fencing then begins to run, gun in hand, up towards the rise.

Back at Little Fidding Church Fortescue's BEST MAN *looks down a little anxiously at the empty pew beside him, while at Carnoustie House ...*

FORTESCUE *completes his spectacular escape from the tower, and racing down to the front door, he sees the empty wagon, looks to either side, then walks quite positively up to it. He climbs surprisingly nimbly aboard, flicks the reins with more courage than skill, and the horse gallops off, nearly sending him flying, through the gates and up the road.*

On the grouse moor the guns and their ladies sit at table drinking champagne. In the background the beaters blow on their hands and wait for their lords and masters.

LORD AMES (raising a glass of champagne to the MAHARAJAH). Much improves the aim, you know . . .

The MAHARAJAH beams.

MAHARAJAH. When I was a young man I could even shoot the Puduni . . .

LORD AMES. What the hell's a Puduni?

MAHARAJAH. Oh, it is a tiny Indian bird . . . Just very small. I could shoot it between beak and ear . . . without damaging either . . . *(Much admiration expressed round the table at this.)* That was when I could still see, of course!

He roars with laughter at this. Everyone else joins in politely, but uncertainly.

LADY AMES. Still drinking?

They look up as she approaches the table. The men stand, except for LORD AMES.

PORTLAND. We've just been discussing what was the smallest thing anyone's ever killed . . .

LADY AMES *(glancing quickly at her husband)*. Oh really . . .

LEICESTER. Newlyn claims to have shot a bluebottle with a twelve bore . . .

Much laughter.

PORTLAND. Didn't kill it though . . . had to finish it off with his foot.

More roars of laughter around the table. LADY AMES *glances quickly up the hill . . .*

LADY AMES. Well . . . are we starting soon . . .?

LORD AMES *(irritably)*. All right! All right!

He holds his glass out the merest fraction and it is immediately filled up by one of the footmen – whose livery is already looking distinctly mud-spattered. He glowers at LADY AMES.

LORD AMES. Since when have you been so keen on shooting . . .?

He drains his glass of champagne. A footman is on the spot to hand him a small linen napkin with which he dabs his mouth.

LORD AMES. A hundred and fifty's my target for the day . . . Must keep ahead of Archie Westminster . . .

SECOND YOUNG MAN *(a consummate creep)*. Oh, I'm sure you'll have no trouble there, sir . . .

LORD AMES *begins to move followed by a gaggle of servants to make sure his coat doesn't fall off, etc. etc.*

LORD AMES. He's ahead of me on pig, rabbit and badger . . . we're level pegging on quail and he can't touch me on tiger, pheasant or rhino . . .

SECOND YOUNG MAN. You've shot rhino sir . . .?

LORD AMES. Only a dozen. Very hard work. Have to get them between the eyes or up the arse. Come on everyone! Into the butts . . .

Meanwhile CORBETT *is nearly at the top of the rise. He's working his way up to the ridge on all fours. He reaches the top and looks down.*

From his vantage point he can see the party dispersing to their butts. CORBETT *moves along until he is in position about four hundred yards behind* LORD AMES's *butt and directly in line with the* MAHARAJAH's.

On a stone track on another part of the moor the carriage with FORTESCUE *aboard careers along only just under control.*

On the main grouse moor the guns and their loaders, and in the MAHARAJAH's *case, the loader and the native guide boy, are taking up positions.*

Guns are checked, dry lips licked, aims taken, hip flasks quickly drained. The chatter and laughter gradually dies down. LADY AMES *enters* LORD AMES's *butt. She looks tight-lipped. Again she looks back up the hill towards her accomplice,* CORBETT. *He has wriggled forward as closely as he can to the front of the ridge.*

LORD AMES *takes a look along his barrel and takes aim.*

CORBETT *takes aim at the back of* LORD AMES. LORD AMES *lowers his rifle and looks round . . .*

In the MAHARAJAH's *butt. The* MAHARAJAH *has a gun up at his shoulder. His boy moves the barrel round to face the direction of the birds. Everyone ducks fearfully.*

FORTESCUE's *horse has finally gone out of control on the road, flinging the carriage onto its side.* FORTESCUE *pulls himself up . . .*

He looks round desperately . . . then he hears a shout:

LORD AMES. Ready Maharajah?

FORTESCUE *races in the direction of the sound, stumbling across the boggy terrain with difficulty, and shouting against the wind.*

FORTESCUE. Stop! Stop!

At Little Fidding the ORGANIST *cranes out of his loft,* FORTESCUE's BEST MAN *is looking very apprehensive. A signal is given by an usher at the door, relayed through another usher to the organist who nods and turns to play. The strains of 'Here Comes the Bride' fill the little church. The* BEST MAN *looks about to wet himself.*

Back at the grouse moor, the MAHARAJAH *shouts from his butt.*

MAHARAJAH. Ready . . . General . . .

LORD AMES. Everyone else ready?

   CORBETT *is at the top of the hill, finger tightening on the trigger.*

   FORTESCUE *is nearby, racing closer.*

   LORD AMES *gives a nod. This is picked up by a head beater who barks the order:*

HEAD BEATER. Drive them out!

   FORTESCUE *appears at this moment behind the butts.*

FORTESCUE. Stop!

But it's too late. A terrific noise is set up by the beaters and FORTESCUE's *voice is drowned . . .*

As fingers tighten on triggers, FORTESCUE *rushes on shouting and waving his arms.*

CORBETT, *higher up on the ridge than* FORTESCUE, *sees him advancing and doesn't know where to aim his gun . . .*

LORD AMES. Here they come!

At the same moment that the air is filled with screeching driven grouse . . .

A surge of organ music heralds the arrival at Little Fidding church of DEBORAH *in all her wedding finery, smiling nervously, on the arm of the* REVEREND FITZBANKS, *and a variety of podgy pageboys and bridesmaids.*

On the grouse moor five hundred miles away LORD AMES *prepares for the slaughter.*

LORD AMES *(with a smile of satisfaction)*. There's some nice fat ones . . . Here we go!

He takes aim, follows the bird, but is just about to fire when he is rugger-tackled to the ground by the flying form of FORTESCUE.

LORD AMES *(furiously)*. What the hell is going on?

He struggles. LADY AMES *looks round, horrified. Up on the ridge* CORBETT's *gun swings wildly.* AMES's *loader joins the struggle.*

FORTESCUE. Get down, sir . . . you're going to be killed.

LORD AMES *(desperately trying to throw* FORTESCUE *off)*. You bloody fool, I'll have you horsewhipped for this . . .

LADY AMES. Leave my husband alone!

She tries to drag the hapless FORTESCUE *away from* AMES.

On the ridge above them, CORBETT'S *finger grasps the trigger.* AMES *pushes* FORTESCUE *to one side. His finger tightens.* FORTESCUE *recovers and hurls* AMES *out of the butt. At the same moment* LADY AMES *flings herself at* FORTESCUE. CORBETT *pulls the trigger. There is a sharp crack.*

At the church DEBORAH *and* FITZBANKS *have reached the chancel steps. They stand there wreathed in smiles, as the organ music reaches a climax.*

On the moor LADY AMES *gasps and falls into* FORTESCUE'S *arms.* FORTESCUE *looks up at the ridge.* CORBETT'S *head appears. Then he gets up, pauses for a moment and, flinging the gun down, starts to run wildly.*

LOADER (*pointing in* CORBETT'S *direction*). Up there!

The MAHARAJAH *moves like lightning. He shouts in Indian to the boy guide, who whips the* MAHARAJAH'S *gun round. The* MAHARAJAH *fires instantly. On the ridge the silhouette of* CORBETT'S *body is frozen still for a minute and then falls backwards. The birds are still flying over and being shot at and at first no one notices what has happened.*

FORTESCUE *is shaking,* LADY AMES *lies in his arms. Slowly the gun fire dies down as more of the party realise what has happened. One or two of them leave their butts and gather round* AMES. *Even the beaters have been stopped. The wind blows.*

The silence on the moor is mirrored back at the church. The organ chords die away, and everyone stands in a tableau, frozen for a moment, waiting.

FORTESCUE *looks down at* LADY AMES *lying in his arms. Her eyes flicker,* FORTESCUE *picks her up. His eyes are full of tears. He looks round at the still stunned and mesmerised sea of faces. Then suddenly he explodes, yelling at them.*

FORTESCUE. Well come on! Do something...

Immediately a couple of beaters run off towards one of the carts. FORTESCUE *picks up* LADY AMES *and carries her across to it. About a dozen of the chinless wonders cluster around* LORD AMES, *helping him up with soothing words.*

At the church, DEBORAH *looks across at the empty* BRIDEGROOM's *pew. The* BEST MAN *spreads his arms helplessly.* FITZBANKS *looks up at the* BISHOP *who waits on the chancel steps to take the service. He shakes his head. They look to the back of the church, hopefully. An usher peers outside, then comes back in and shakes his head.*

On the grouse moor LORD AMES *is being helped away.* FORTESCUE *carries* LADY AMES *and lays her in the back of a cart. Two beaters and a wagon driver come across to help.*

FORTESCUE *(to one of the beaters).* Take her home...

WAGON DRIVER. It's not my wagon, sir...

FORTESCUE *(furiously).* Take her home...!

The WAGON DRIVER *snaps into action.*

FORTESCUE *(to* LADY AMES*).* You'll be all right.

LADY AMES *(in obvious pain).* Oh yes, I'm sure, Corbett's such a bloody awful shot...

FORTESCUE. I'm sorry... dear God, I'm sorry...

LADY AMES *stretches out her hand towards him.*

LADY AMES. You were only trying to do the decent thing... *(She smiles at this.)* That's the trouble with you, Charles, far too decent...

LADY AMES' *face tenses with discomfort as the driver jumps on to the front of the wagon.*

LADY AMES. I got it all wrong, didn't I?

The wagon jerks into motion.

FORTESCUE *(keeping up with it).* What do you mean...?

LADY AMES *manages a smile as the wagon bumps off across the rough moorland.*

LADY AMES. I tried to convert the missionary...

FORTESCUE *just stares after her as the wagon disappears. A voice shouts out from behind.*

VOICE. Hey!

FORTESCUE *turns. The* DUKE OF PORTLAND *advances holding out a pudgy hand.*

PORTLAND. Well done! You've saved the old boy's life.

FORTESCUE's *eyes meet* PORTLAND's. *Then* FORTESCUE *draws his thin and crumpled black clerical jacket around him and turns and walks away...*

The Rectory at Little Fidding. Some days later. At a table DEBORAH *sits surrounded by neat files of papers. She scans through a letter she has just written. She is quite happy, doing what she enjoys best...*

DEBORAH *(writing).* Dear Mr and Mrs Campion, Thank you so much for the wedding present which I herewith regretfully return, Yours sincerely... *(Here she signs briskly and efficiently.)* ... Deborah Fitzbanks... *(She pauses for a moment and adds)* ... Miss. *(She stamps the letter and puts it carefully on a pile of others, picking up another as she does so.)* Dear Lady Fermleigh, Thank you so much for the wedding present which I herewith regretfully return, Yours sincerely...

She looks up at the sound of a light tap on the door. It's PARSWELL, *the odd-job man.*

PARSWELL. What you want done with these please, Miss...?

He comes into the room a little way and she sees that he is thrusting one of Fortescue's tribal objects at her. DEBORAH *peers at it. She stands and comes to take a closer look.*

DEBORAH. What is it?

PARSWELL. I'm not rightly sure ma'am... I found it under the bed.

DEBORAH *runs her fingers lightly over the smooth rounded shining surface of the object... then she runs her hand back up the object again. She smiles and murmurs appreciatively. She looks at* PARSWELL. *He smiles back, a little awkwardly.*

DEBORAH. You look nice with your hair like that, Parswell...

NARRATOR: After the shooting of Lady Ames, or the Rescue of Lord Ames, as it became known, Fortescue returned to the Mission he loved, and which had loved him. So successful was he at filling it with girls that in March 1907 the Bishop of London himself closed it down.

The Mission House interior, empty now, the beds broken and askew. A rumble is heard in the distance and a religious picture on the wall has begun to shake. There is a crash and the picture glass is shattered as the wall behind it collapses spectacularly, under a demolisher's ball and chain.

Dust rises. A foreman's whistle blows.

Dockland. On the mud flats. December 1907.

NARRATOR. The Bishop now offered Fortescue a simple choice: to stay in Dockland or to stay in the Church. He chose to stay in Dockland. And though he never wore a dog-collar again he was known to the end of his life as 'the Missionary'.

FORTESCUE, *without his dog-collar, is discovered rooting around amidst the flotsam and jetsam of the shore line. He picks up and tosses an old piece of wood into a barrow. Helping him are some of the girls from the Mission –* EMMELINE *and* NINA, *and another, with their skirts hitched up and tied in a bundle round their waists. He grabs one more piece of driftwood and slings it on the barrow. As he walks towards the barrow he shouts to three boys who are playing ducks and drakes beside the river.*

FORTESCUE. Come on you lazy beggars! Give a hand!

The boys turn and come running over. They all grab one handle of the barrow.

FORTESCUE. Not all on the same one!

Shouting and laughing the boys start to push the barrow whilst FORTESCUE, EMMELINE *and* NINA *follow on.*

BOY. What's all this for, Rev?

FORTESCUE. So we can patch up that place at the end of the road and you can have somewhere to muck around in.

BOY. Will it be a Mission?

FORTESCUE (*after a pause, grins down at him*). No, just somewhere to muck around in.

One of his female helpers hangs behind tugging at some large object stuck in the mud.

FORTESCUE. Come on, we're *going* . . .

She looks up from her efforts. Beneath the sweat and grime, the eyes shine unmistakably, ISABEL – LADY AMES.

ISABEL *(shouting back)*. I can't move this on my own.

FORTESCUE. Well, leave it . . .

This goads ISABEL *into superhuman effort. She heaves the precious object out of the mud and drags it off to the barrow, with a look of deep satisfaction.*

The barrow continues on its way.

FORTESCUE *and his procession make their way through the East End. He is happy again, as he hasn't been since he left Africa. At one point the procession arrives at the site of the old Mission. There is a brand new building in its place now. The signboard on it reads 'THE McEVOY COMPANY — YELLOW WHIPPET BRAND'.*

Over the last two or three group shots, we lose the colour and the picture becomes sepia. We freeze the sepia picture. This leads us to a series of faded photographs of FORTESCUE *and* ISABEL *revealed to be in an album. It is being read under a school desk, surreptitiously.*

A SCHOOLMASTER'S VOICE. Put that away, Fortescue!

A small schoolboy's hand snaps the book shut and puts it into a desk
. . . the desk lid comes down.
Darkness.

THE END

After the Story:

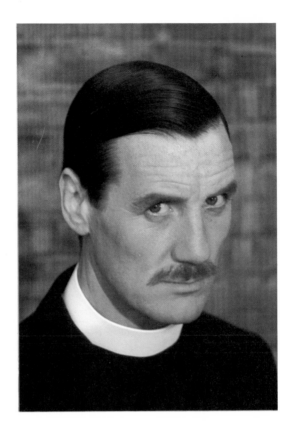

CHARLES FORTESCUE
was de-frocked in December 1906 and his Mission was converted
into a chemical warehouse for McEvoy's 'Yellow Whippet' Lemon
Tonic Company. But Fortescue himself stayed on in Dockland. He
used his experience gained in Africa to become an accomplished
carpenter, builder and entertainer. His Samburu war dance was a
star turn at the Frog and Postman and it was performed in full with
the help of the Salvation Army Band and the Isle of Dogs Ballet
School at the Coronation in 1910. FORTESCUE and his wife Isabel
became much-loved characters in London's East End and he was
still known as 'The Rev' when he died there, in a snake charming
accident, in 1933.

LADY ISABEL AMES

recovered from her wounds on the grouse moor after her husband
had bought a hospital for her, to try and prevent any scandal. Once
it was clear that she intended to divorce him he cut her off without a
penny in which state she arrived in London to join Charles
Fortescue in April 1907. For the first time since she had given up
being plain Isabel Dogmore – 'The Fastest in the Business' she was
happy – drinking again at the Frog and Postman in Rotherhithe,
watching legendary East End characters like 'Mad Dick' Poncraine,
the Burning Spoon Player, and joining in the life she wished she'd
never left. She lived to be a hundred and three and died of shock in
1962.

THE FIRST LORD AMES OF MORETONHAMPSTEAD
became more and more interested in politics. Between 1906 and
1912 he put no less than 40 unsuccessful bills before the House of
Lords. Among them were: *The Selective Killings Bill*, designed to have
people executed before they had committed a crime, thus catching
murderers before they had a chance to become murderers; *The Very
Rich People's Protection Bill*: to introduce government assistance for
anyone who could prove beyond reasonable doubt that they had
more than four homes; *The Alleyway Tax*: a tax on all those with
nowhere to sleep – based on how much of the alleyway they took up;
The Edible Orphans Bill (1909); *The Abolition of Poverty Bill* (1910) –
rejected on the grounds of the amount of explosive involved; *The
Needy Employment Bill*: advocating the use of the needy as tunnel
supports on the new London Underground.

LORD AMES died in his study in 1912 whilst testing a less humane
method of garotting.

DEBORAH FITZBANKS

became best known as the inventor of the Fitzbanks 'Easi-File'
which did so much to win the First World War for Britain. Shortly
after being abandoned by Fortescue she fell in love with and married
Oliver St John Parswell – the Fitzbanks' odd-job man. He was so
odd in fact that she spent most of her later years nursing him back to
health after he had attacked a wall in North London. They had two
children whom DEBORAH called A and B.

REVEREND FITZBANKS
became a prominent churchman and wrote many religious
pamphlets including *Bee-Keeping for Vicars*, *A Protestant's Guide to Home
Cider-Making*, and *The Single Clergyman's Book of Home Preserves*. As an
acknowledgement of the debt owed to him by the church he was
transferred from Little Fidding to Tiny Fidding in June 1909.

THE BISHOP OF LONDON

After his lack of success with the Mission to Fallen Women, he turned his attention to the foundation of a Mission to Fallen Men – open to mountaineers who'd dropped over 7000 feet. He also pioneered a Mission to Scrum-Halves and wrote a special hymn for squash players . . . 'Oh little ball we smite thee'. With the publication of his book *Jesus and Sport* in 1923 he became an overnight celebrity and left to become the first Bishop of Hollywood in January of 1924.

He fell through a fissure in the Earth's surface in 1937.

SLATTERTHWAITE
retired from the Ames' service at the outbreak of the Great War. He
had found the pressure of his work increasingly arduous and in 1911
he had lost the young King George V for three hours in the
shrubbery and a prominent Belgian aristocrat – Count
Schwartzhaven – was lost altogether between the bathroom and the
North-West wing, and has never been found. In 1915 Slatterthwaite
began work on his authoritative manual for butlers *How To Find A
Room From 4 Feet Away.*

Always a keen traveller, SLATTERTHWAITE was last seen in
Southern Lebanon on the way home from London to his house in
Dorking.

Roll of Honour

DIRECTED BY	Richard Loncraine
EXECUTIVE PRODUCERS	George Harrison and Denis O'Brien
PRODUCED BY	Neville C. Thompson and Michael Palin
SCREENPLAY BY	Michael Palin
ART DIRECTOR	Norman Garwood
LIGHTING CAMERAMAN	Peter Hannan
SOUND RECORDIST	Tony Jackson
COSTUME DESIGNER	Shuna Harwood
EDITOR	Paul Green
MAKE-UP SUPERVISOR	Ken Lintott
HAIRDRESSING SUPERVISOR	Ramon Gow
PROPERTY MASTER	George Ball
CONSTRUCTION MANAGER	Peter Verard
ELECTRICAL GAFFER	Robert (Chuck) Finch
PRODUCTION MANAGER	Graham Ford
LOCATION MANAGER	Joanna Gollins
PRODUCTION ASSISTANT	Norma Garment
ASSISTANT DIRECTOR	Gary White
SECOND ASSISTANT DIRECTOR	Bobbie Wright
THIRD ASSISTANT DIRECTOR	Derek Harrington
THIRD ASSISTANT DIRECTOR	Chris Thompson
CONTINUITY	Alison Thorne
CASTING DIRECTOR	Irene Lamb
ASSISTANT TO THE PRODUCERS	Kathy Sykes
ASSISTANT TO THE DIRECTOR	Maria Apodiacos
PRODUCTION ACCOUNTANT	Bobby (R. J.) Blues
ASSISTANT PRODUCTION ACCOUNTANT	Anthony Coroon
ASSISTANT ART DIRECTOR	Keith Pain
SECOND ASSISTANT ART DIRECTOR	Maggie Gray
SET DRESSER	Ian Whittaker
PRODUCTION BUYER	Leslie Fulford

DECOR ARTIST	Norman Hart
CAMERA OPERATOR	Dewi Humphreys
FOCUS	Colin Davidson
CLAPPER/LOADER	Stefan Stanowski
GRIP	Collin Manning
CAMERA CAR DRIVER	Alan Rank
BOOM OPERATOR	John Ralph
SOUND MAINTENANCE	Clive Osborne
WARDROBE SUPERVISOR	Keith Denny
WARDROBE ASSISTANT	Rosemary Worth
WARDROBE ASSISTANT	Frank Vinall
MAKE-UP ARTIST	Sandra Exelby
HAIRDRESSER	Ronnie Cogan
ASSISTANT EDITOR	Elaine Thomas
SECOND ASSISTANT EDITOR	Karen Baker
SOUND EDITOR	Ron Davis
ASSISTANT SOUND EDITOR	Chris Ackland
DUBBING MIXER	Gerry Humphreys
PUBLICIST	Wendy Tayler
STILLS PHOTOGRAPHER	David Farrell
DRAPES	Ron Cowan
CHARGEHAND DRESSING PROP	Les Benson
DRESSING PROPERTYMAN	Barry Arnold
DRESSING PROPERTYMAN	John Chisholm
STAND-BY CHARGEHAND PROPERTYMAN	Denis Hopperton
STAND-BY PROPERTYMAN	Peter Benson
PROP STOREMAN	Stan Cook
PROPERTYMAN	Edward Francis
PROPERTYMAN	Frank B. Marks
STAND-BYS	
CARPENTER	Craig Hillier
PAINTER	Alan Grenham
STAGEHAND	Clive Rivers
RIGGER	Richard Harris

CONSTRUCTION DEPARTMENT	Lee Aspey
	Gerald Devlin
	Brian Higgins
	W. P. (Bill) Lyons
	R. Lane
	K. J. Small
	Michael Fisher
	Edward King
	N. A. Fletcher
	Gary Hedges
	John McGuigan
	Charles McGinlay
	B. Mason
	David B. Wicks
	Ken Powell
	W. J. Burke
	Denis Murray
	Dennis Wraight
	Dave Wiggins
	Peter Hawkins
	Harry Heeks
	John Martin
	Roy O'Connor
	Larry Marchant
	Frank Berlin
	Graham Bullock
	F. Adam
	Harold Burst
	Chris Flanagan
	Richard Stachini
ELECTRICAL DEPARTMENT	George Hunt
	Ray Coates
	Alan Macpherson
	Larry Randall
	Richie Seal
	Les Weighell
UNIT DRIVERS	Brian Brookner
	Tony Hocking
UNIT NURSE	Petra Walters
LOCATION CATERERS	THE LOCATION CATERERS LTD.
	Phil Hobbs
	Len Nieder
	Mark Kingston
	Fred Gaida
	Rex Payton

The cast

REVEREND FORTESCUE	Michael Palin
LADY AMES	Maggie Smith
LORD AMES	Trevor Howard
THE BISHOP	Denholm Elliott
SLATTERTHWAITE	Michael Hordern
REVEREND FITZBANKS	Graham Crowden
CORBETT	David Suchet
DEBORAH	Phoebe Nicholls
ADA	Tricia George
EMMELINE	Valerie Whittington
LORD FERMLEIGH	Roland Culver
LADY FERMLEIGH	Rosamund Greenwood
PARSWELL	Timothy Spall
SINGER IN GIN PALACE	Neil Innes
OLD MAN OUTSIDE BROTHEL	John Barrett
Mission Girls	Dawn Archibald
	Frances Barber
	Debbie Bishop
	Ceri Jackson
	Janine Lesley
	Sasha Mitchell
	Francine Morgan
	Sophie Thompson
	Sally Watkins
Small Boys at Mudflats	Tony Fawcett
	Jaime Barr
	Edward Bumstead
ARTHUR PIMP	David Leland
EMILY	Anne-Marie Marriott
USHER AT WEDDING	Hugh Fraser
BEST MAN AT WEDDING	Peter Bourke
MILLICENT	Janine Duvitski
FERMLEIGH'S MAID	Tilly Vosburgh
FERMLEIGH'S BUTLER	Arthur Howard
FERMLEIGH'S DOCTOR	Hugh Walters
FIRST SILLY ARISTOCRAT	Julian Curry

SECOND SILLY ARISTOCRAT	Charles McKeown
MAHARAJAH	Ishaq Bux
LORD QUIMBY	Tony Steedman
LADY QUIMBY	Damaris Hayman
YOUNG MAN	David Dixon
YOUNG MAN	Anton Lesser
SIR CYRIL EVERIDGE	Frank Mills
MAHARAJAH'S BOY	Yussef Shah

Special thanks are due to CHRISTOPHER THYNNE and all at Longleat House for their enormous help.